Dirty Story

and Other Plays

Dirty Story

and Other Plays

John Patrick Shanley

Theatre Communications Group
New York
2007

This publication is made possible in part with public funds from the New York State Council on the Arts, a State Agency.

TCG books are exclusively distributed to the book trade by Consortium Book Sales and Distribution, 1045 Westgate Drive, St. Paul, MN 55114.

LIBRARY OF CONGRESS CATALOGING-IN-PUBLICATION DATA

Shanley, John Patrick.
Dirty story and other plays / by John Patrick Shanley.—1st ed.
p. cm.
ISBN 13: 978-1-55936-282-5
ISBN 10: 1-55936-282-0
I. Title.
PS3569.H3337A6   2006
812'.54—dc22   2006030924

Cover design by John Gall
Cover photo © Craig Aurness/CORBIS
Author photo by Monique Carboni
Book design and composition by Lisa Govan

First Edition, May 2007

Contents

Dirty Story

This play is dedicated to Professor Terence Patrick Moran,
a tremendous enemy of bullshit.

Production History

Dirty Story was originally produced by the LAByrinth Theater Company (John Ortiz and Philip Seymour Hoffman, Co-Artistic Directors; Oliver Dow, Executive Director; Robin Kramer and John Gould Rubin, Producers; Stephanie Yankwitt, Associate Producer) in New York City, opening on February 18, 2003. It was directed by John Patrick Shanley; the set design was by Michelle Malavet, the lighting design was by Jeremy Morris, the sound design was by Elizabeth Rhodes, the costume design was by Mimi O'Donnell and the stage manager was Mary E. Leach. The cast was as follows:

BRUTUS	David Deblinger
WANDA	Florencia Lozano
FRANK	Chris McGarry
LAWRENCE/WATSON	Michael Puzzo

Characters

Brutus
Wanda
Frank
Lawrence/Watson

Place

New York City.

Time

The present.

Act One

Scene 1

Music: Mongo Santamaria's take on "Watermelon Man." A park. Two outdoor chess tables. A trash can. A little bench, center. Brutus is drinking coffee, playing a game of chess alone. Across the way, another man, an aging English patrician, Lawrence, also plays chess alone; he's listening to music on a headset. Lawrence raises a sign which reads: FICTION. He lowers it. The music segues into street sounds. Wanda enters. She's pulling a six-foot palm tree in a luggage carrier. She approaches Lawrence.

WANDA: Mister Chiappa? Brutus Chiappa?

LAWRENCE: I don't even want to be here.

WANDA: I'm sure you don't.

LAWRENCE: I just want to go home.

WANDA: I'm sure you do. But are you . . . *("Brutus Chiappa?")*

LAWRENCE *(Overlapping)*: Please! I just want to go home to my chair, my dog, and my mother!

WANDA: You're not Brutus Chiappa, are you?

LAWRENCE: No.

BRUTUS: Are you Wanda?

WANDA: Yes?

BRUTUS: I think you want me. I'm Brutus.

WANDA: Oh. Hi. I'm Wanda. *(To Lawrence)* Sorry.

LAWRENCE: I just want to go home. And I'm going to go home in a little bit.

BRUTUS: Never mind him. He has nothing to do with anything.

WANDA: Brutus?

BRUTUS: Yes.

WANDA: Oh, I'm sorry. There's no picture on your book jackets.

BRUTUS: It's not worthy of further explanation.

WANDA: Nice to meet you.

BRUTUS: You have a large plant.

WANDA: Yeah, good buy on Sixth Avenue. It's all the real estate I can afford. Am I interrupting something?

BRUTUS: Nothing to be done about it.

WANDA: I could come back.

BRUTUS: That's ridiculous.

WANDA: I just noticed you're playing a game of chess.

BRUTUS: Yeah.

WANDA *(Indicating Lawrence)*: He is, too.

BRUTUS: I don't know that man. We just happen to be sharing a public space.

WANDA: Is it something people do now? Play chess alone? In proximity to other people playing chess alone?

BRUTUS: I don't know what people do. I can only speak for myself. I like to play alone.

WANDA: It seems funny. I mean two people who want to play chess so close by each other. Seems silly they're not in the same game.

BRUTUS: Simply because two people are physically near each other doesn't mean they should be friends.

WANDA: Chess isn't about friendship, it's about combat.

BRUTUS: Even conflict requires common ground. Come on, sit down. I don't like to look up at people.

WANDA: Oh, of course. I'm sorry. Thank you. *(Sits)* I have been deeply affected by your poetry, your essays, your books for a long time now. Thank you for agreeing to meet with me.

BRUTUS: I don't mind meeting. I'll go to meetings. I'm willing to meet with anybody. Have you heard different or something?

WANDA: No. I just want to acknowledge that it's an act of generosity to take the time to give a graduate student the benefit of your experience.

BRUTUS *(Rummaging in a valise)*: You seem a little old to be a graduate student. I was out of graduate school and established in the world by the time I was . . . How old are you?

WANDA: I'm still quite young.

(Brutus pulls a manuscript out of his bag, gets up with his coffee.)

BRUTUS: By the time I was twenty-six. Here. *(Hands her the manuscript and heads for the trash can)*

WANDA: For some of us, being a student is a lifelong occupation.

BRUTUS: I have a nephew like that. His parents are suicidal. *(Throws his coffee lid in the trash)*

WANDA: I didn't mean I don't work. I pay my way.

BRUTUS: You don't get a little scholarship money or something? A little subsidy?

WANDA: Some. It's based on merit.

BRUTUS: You're a tomboy.

WANDA: What?

BRUTUS: All right, all right. I read your . . . What do you call it? A homily? *(Sits on the bench)*

WANDA: A novel.

(He pours his coffee into the palm tree. She reacts.)

BRUTUS: It was wretched, it was ignominious, it was a shonda. I lament that you wrote it. It takes seventeen trees to make one ton of paper. You might think about that the next time you consider writing.

WANDA: Oh, I'm sorry if it wasn't good.

BRUTUS: It wasn't good.

WANDA: Could you clarify in what way it wasn't good?

(He gets up.)

BRUTUS: Don't you read the paper? Hasn't anybody told you the news?

WANDA: What?

BRUTUS: Fiction is dead. *(Tosses his empty cup in the trash)*

WANDA: You don't really believe that.

BRUTUS: Fiction is a fabrication. A lie. An unfounded fantasy. We're not interested anymore. We don't care. We don't want to suspend our disbelief. Fiction is dead.

WANDA: But then what's alive?

BRUTUS: Nonfiction.

WANDA: All fiction is dead and all nonfiction without limitation is alive?

BRUTUS: Correct. But all nonfiction is not of interest. One wishes to be in some sense surprised. The pages should set off a border skirmish. "I knew that but I didn't know I knew it." That kind of thing.

(Brutus wanders over to Lawrence's game and steals a peek. Lawrence covers his game.)

LAWRENCE: Oh no you don't!

BRUTUS *(Making an answering gesture)*: Oh yes I do!

(He swings back to his table and seat.)

We want work which is both credible *and* fantastic. In short, it should smack of accuracy, but fall short or long of agreed-upon truth. Like plausible gossip.

WANDA: I've always thought of gossip as a social evil.

BRUTUS: It holds a potent fascination.

WANDA: For the mob.

BRUTUS: Sometimes the mob is on to something.

WANDA: What about your book *Understanding Japanese*?

BRUTUS: What about it?

WANDA: That was nonfiction. Is that an example of this un-agreed-upon truth?

BRUTUS: Doesn't interest me anymore.

WANDA: Why not?

BRUTUS: I was writing about fashion in Japan acting as a substitute for rage. The Eastern idea of face recast as the Western idea

of the individual. Unfortunately, the subject matter, by definition, confined me to appearances.

WANDA: It was a wonderful book.

BRUTUS: I'm through with it! And I'm through with the Japanese!

WANDA: May I ask why?

BRUTUS: Their last great idea was the kamikaze.

WANDA: That's offensive.

BRUTUS: The truth usually is. Modern Japan is karaoke.

WANDA: You like to provoke.

BRUTUS: I like to poke open assumptions and let the stink out.

WANDA: But if your book wasn't nonfiction, what was it? Sort of an
essay?

BRUTUS: An essay? Look. Your novel is no good.

WANDA *(Explodes)*: GOD . . . *(Controls)* dammit! You poured coffee
into my tree!

BRUTUS: Yes. Your book is one of those utopian fantasies founded
on an insanely optimistic view of human beings.

WANDA: Don't you think we should aim high?

BRUTUS: Not if you want to hit something.

WANDA: But what if I want to envision something new, something
that doesn't exist, and by describing it, set in motion its genesis?

BRUTUS: Like Karl Marx?

WANDA: In a way.

LAWRENCE: Karl Marx.

BRUTUS: Oh ho, you woke him up. Look at that. Another English lefty.
Probably thinks Joe Stalin was a boy scout. *(To Lawrence)* You
ever hear of the gulag, you hamhock!?

LAWRENCE: Absolutely! No humidity.

(Brutus looks from Lawrence to Wanda like: Am I alone here?)

WANDA: You can't fool me. I know you have ideals. What about your
books of poetry?

BRUTUS: I've sworn off. There's a reason the poet's instrument is the
lyre.

WANDA: The ideal is important. There's a mindless momentum that
comes out of the past. The counteracting force is idealism.
I wrote this book to change the course of things.

BRUTUS: Too bad it doesn't have a plot.

WANDA: No, it doesn't have a plot. It *is* a plot, the blueprint for a dream. At one time, a man imagined the Taj Mahal, then people built it, now it exists. That's what I want to do.

BRUTUS: You've let your imagination pollute your aesthetic.

WANDA: Imagination is the future's workshop.

BRUTUS: Listen to me. Never write a book like this again. Confine yourself to nonfiction. Better yet, restrict yourself to reading. Your manuscript has no understanding of the possible, much less the real. Furthermore, it's a gloss on a gloss. An utterly unoriginal, very long "What If?" You want me to sloganize it for you? It's all sugar and no shit.

WANDA: You don't have to be vulgar.

BRUTUS *(Makes a smoothing gesture)*: How do you know?

WANDA: Restless?

BRUTUS: Always.

WANDA: I can fix the book.

BRUTUS: You can burn the book.

WANDA: There's a real need behind this work! Maybe I haven't found the right words yet, but they exist in my heart and I will find a way to say them!

BRUTUS: Big feelings are not the same as big ideas.

WANDA: Display some doubt, would you? You would benefit from exhibiting some doubt.

BRUTUS: Really? I don't think so. I suggest you go home.

WANDA: I'll never give up.

BRUTUS: Go home, chickadee.

WANDA: I will be heard.

BRUTUS: Wipe the spittle off your face, take up a new hobby.

WANDA: No.

BRUTUS: No one wants to hear from you what should happen in life. How they should live. You do not have a better idea. This book is dead.

WANDA: Then I'll write another one. Don't you understand? I don't care about the book. I care about the thing behind it.

BRUTUS: And what's that?

WANDA: Me! There has to be a place for me! In life. Where I can speak and where I am heard. And I believe there are people who want to hear what I have to say. Even if you're not one of them. Even if I don't know what it is that I have to say yet. So maybe you're right on this one, okay? Let's say you're absolutely right. This book is a piece of shit. If that's the case, *(Throws it in the trash can)* it's chucked.

BRUTUS: You've managed to surprise me. This is how you respond to a destructive critic? Are you a masochist?

WANDA: I want to improve myself and I'm willing to pay the price.

BRUTUS: What are you, German?

WANDA: I, well, it's . . . Actually, I am German, of German descent, on both sides. How did you know that?

BRUTUS: I was joking. But obviously humor has less wit than blood. I would've thought you were a Jew.

WANDA: No one thinks I'm a Jew. I am a Jew.

BRUTUS: A German Jew.

WANDA: What are you?

BRUTUS: I'm a Jew German. So why did you make this 348-page mud pie?

WANDA: I think of it as a folktale.

BRUTUS: Folktales beguile.

WANDA: Why did you agree to meet me if you thought so little of it?

BRUTUS: I had to get out of the house. My work drives me mad.

WANDA: But there must've been something in it that you thought valuable in some small way?

BRUTUS: I liked one word in your cover letter.

WANDA: What was it?

BRUTUS: "Damsel." You used the word "damsel."

WANDA: I was actually ashamed that I used that word. I thought it was a bit coy.

BRUTUS: Coy as in "charm"? You were trying to charm me?

WANDA: Well, yes.

BRUTUS: Looking over your fan like some crafty contessa? Dropping your handkerchief. Using this medieval word and this oblique tone to get what you wanted.

WANDA: That's right.

BRUTUS: Which is what?

WANDA: I was trying to arouse your chivalry. So you would want to help me.

BRUTUS: My chivalry. So you're a romantic.

WANDA: Somewhat.

BRUTUS: A perilous, perilous thing to be.

(She turns to steel for a moment.)

WANDA: It has power, too.

(A pause.)

LAWRENCE: Excuse me.

WANDA *(To Lawrence)*: Yes?

(Brutus grabs her wrist to hold her attention. She looks at his hand on her wrist.)

BRUTUS: And has this use of medieval mythology worked for you in the past?

WANDA: No, actually, it never has.

BRUTUS: So that's why you were ashamed you used the word "damsel" in your letter. You were mortified to be using a ploy which had already proved itself a bust. It's like you never learn.

WANDA *(Removing his hand)*: But I do learn.

(A pause.)

LAWRENCE: Excuse me.

WANDA: Yes?

LAWRENCE: Do you have the time?

BRUTUS: It's twelve o'clock.

LAWRENCE: I'll be leaving soon.

BRUTUS: I can't wait.

LAWRENCE: You'll miss me when I'm gone.

BRUTUS: I doubt that.

WANDA: You say you don't know that man?

BRUTUS: That's right. He's just some misplaced duffer, one of those types that show up in the park and like to oversee everything. *(Calls to Lawrence)* Right, Pop?

LAWRENCE *(Indicating his headset)*: Mozart.

WANDA: I think you're just testy because . . . Are you working on something now that's frustrating?

BRUTUS: Your blue jeans make me laugh.

WANDA: Why?

BRUTUS: The intelligentsia attempting to identify with the worker. Chairman Mao couture. A vestige of the '60s. But you want service, don't you?

WANDA: Have you looked at this theory that we're all descended from seven mothers?

BRUTUS: I'm aware of it.

WANDA: What do you think?

BRUTUS: I think the man who formulated that theory was a eunuch.

WANDA: Oh, come on. He was a scientist propounding a scientific idea.

BRUTUS: The idea that we're all descended from seven mothers is not a scientific idea. It's a political idea.

WANDA: And you don't like the politics.

BRUTUS: I don't like politics masquerading as science any more than I care for aggression disguised as dialogue.

WANDA: What are you talking about?

BRUTUS: You.

WANDA: Me?

BRUTUS: Seven mothers. You're interfering with my work. *(He starts gathering up his chess pieces)*

WANDA: How?

BRUTUS: This is why I need isolation.

WANDA: I would think an informed exchange could only be useful.

BRUTUS: You don't understand who you're dealing with.

WANDA: You said your work was driving you mad.

BRUTUS: It is. *(Stops collecting his chess pieces)* I'm chasing an idea, but it runs from me like a truant.

WANDA: What's the idea?

BRUTUS: Story.

WANDA: Story?

(Brutus gestures and gestures again as he speaks, as if smoothing down chaos or casting a spell.)

BRUTUS: Storytelling as a force. Storytelling as an invasive, itinerant, organizing principle. Like the Roman army. Story invades experience, reshapes it into its own cultural likeness, and then moves on. Another analogy. This one agricultural. Cotton farming. Storytelling is like cotton farming. A voracious crop that depletes the soil. It uses up one field after another. Poetry. Drama. The novel. The movie. Each medium exploited to the point of exhaustion, and then dropped. My question: When will this storytelling impulse stop eroding forms and itself become bankrupt? Is that happening now? If so, what follows? And perhaps most importantly, what will be the effect on the biggest story of all? History. If Story abandons History, will we come to imagine History in other terms? Or is History, as the Germans so recently declared, dead?

WANDA: Wow. Ambitious stuff.

BRUTUS: By "ambitious," do you mean grandiose?

WANDA: Not in a pejorative sense.

BRUTUS: That's the umbrella idea. You can't address all of any umbrella at once. You've got to go spoke by spoke. I'm thinking smaller at the moment. An illustration. Something which pertains.

WANDA: What?

BRUTUS: Melodrama.

(Lawrence stands abruptly, sweeps his chess pieces into a box.)

LAWRENCE: Melodrama! Melodrama! Is that painted whore out about swishing her scarlet skirt again? Not on my watch. I've had a bellyful of that wench. You're on your own. Good-bye. *(He exits)*

WANDA: I guess he's not a fan of melodrama.

(Brutus crosses to Lawrence's table and starts to unpack his chess pieces, setting up Lawrence's endgame.)

BRUTUS: He just likes to slip on his own bar of soap.

WANDA: What are you doing?

BRUTUS: He was at my table.

WANDA: Oh. So you're interested in the storytelling impulse as manifested in melodrama?

BRUTUS: Yes.

WANDA: What do you mean by "melodrama" exactly? You mean like soap opera?

BRUTUS: No, not like soap opera. Soap opera is a late unrobust example of what I mean. A better model would be the serial. *The Perils of Pauline.*

WANDA: Wasn't that a movie?

BRUTUS: Early silent film. 1914. Girl tied to the railroad tracks by a villain. Train coming. It contains the archetypes I need. The Villain and the Victim.

WANDA: So it's sort of raw, unsophisticated . . .

BRUTUS: Popular. Exactly.

WANDA: I wouldn't think that would interest you. It's so . . . unrooted.

BRUTUS: No, your work is unrooted. *The Perils of Pauline* is rooted.

WANDA: In what?

BRUTUS: Originally, human behavior. Now, human mythology. Even genetic memory.

WANDA: So she's tied to the tracks by this villain, the train is coming. And what happens then?

BRUTUS: I don't care about the rest of it.

WANDA: But what happens?

BRUTUS: She's saved.

WANDA: By who?

BRUTUS: A cowboy or something. Cuts her loose, kills the Villain or something.

WANDA: So there's a hero.

BRUTUS: Not interested in a hero.

WANDA: But isn't the hero an archetype, too? The Villain, the Victim, and the Hero.

BRUTUS: In my view, the hero is only an interruption. For my purposes, there is no hero.

WANDA: But then won't she just get squashed by the train?

BRUTUS: Is that what you think happens?

WANDA: Not necessarily, I suppose. I think, if you were to look at it as a fairy tale, it might be about a change in perception. The male figure, initially viewed by the woman as a threat, transforms into a positive figure as a result of emotional crisis. The train.

BRUTUS: There are two people in this story. Everything isn't an extension of your ego.

WANDA: I know that.

BRUTUS: All problems aren't solved by negotiating with yourself.

WANDA: I didn't say they were.

BRUTUS: Obviously, you've never been married.

WANDA: But actually, I have.

BRUTUS: I trust it did not end well.

WANDA: No, it didn't.

BRUTUS: Men aren't dreams that women have. There weren't seven mothers and no fathers. Men exist separately from your need for them. We aren't lessons for you to learn. We aren't mistakes you make or don't make. We are worlds, we are countries, and we have our ways.

WANDA: I'm aware that you exist.

BRUTUS: As I relate to you.

WANDA: Exclusive of me.

BRUTUS: Why did you send me that awful book?

WANDA: I didn't know it was awful. Do you really mean that you agreed to meet me on the basis of one word in my *cover letter*?

BRUTUS: Yes.

WANDA: And that word was "damsel"?

BRUTUS: "Damsel" is a melodramatic icon.

WANDA: Are you somewhat nuts?

BRUTUS: Only to the frogs, my dear. Are you a frog? Do you want to have ideas that legitimately unspool from within? Or are you content to sit on your lilypad believing that you are having thoughts when what you are actually having are belches caused by swallowing undigested chunks of culture?! Originality is not for frogs croaking in chorus. I'll tell you something real. Originality is soul. Every era has its words. There's a word around these days. Authenticity. People are looking for authenticity. It's just the latest word. People are looking for their souls. They climb mountains looking for it, go into the desert, mingle with the destitute. Enter tombs. You think I'm crazy? You've just joined the villagers chasing Dr. Franken-

stein's monster up the hill. There was a movie! And no one
understood it. Those villagers were the Nazis. And what was
the Creature? The Creature was Soul. "It's monstrous! Kill it!"
Maybe they were right. But they started a fire in the castle
that's burning still. That's it. I've gotta go.

WANDA: But the monster killed a little girl!

BRUTUS: Is that what you think happened?

WANDA: Isn't it?

BRUTUS: I've got to go.

WANDA: But we've just started talking!

BRUTUS: I have to get back to my writing. I haven't written a word all
day. I realize in talking to you, I am squandering something that
could be part of my work. I can't afford to talk anymore.

WANDA: Please! This always happens to me.

BRUTUS: What?

WANDA: Everyone wants to get away from me. Nobody likes me. It's
the story of my life.

BRUTUS: Do you think I'm popular?

WANDA: Compared to me, yes.

BRUTUS: I doubt that.

(She rushes to the trash can, retrieves her manuscript.)

WANDA: I want to understand why my book is bad.

BRUTUS: Look in the mirror. Good-bye.

WANDA: I'll call you.

BRUTUS: Don't.

WANDA: Thank you for talking to me.

BRUTUS: Only a German Jew could say that.

*(He grabs her manuscript and throws it on the ground. He goes.
Music: Richard Harris singing "MacArthur Park." She starts to
pick up the scattered pages. The scene change takes place
around her. She clutches the pages to her bosom, then makes a
decision, and throws it in the trash. Makes a balletic move to
express her frustration and longing. Circles her palm tree like a
ballerina, rolls it, looks through its fronds as if a sad jungle girl.
Then tips it onto her back, and slowly walks off. As . . .)*

Scene 2

Brutus enters his apartment with a glass of wine and opens one of three large shuttered windows. Behind the shutter, the sash is open. The music continues. It's a loft space. An old metal ladder, an old movie studio light on wheels. A metal wardrobe, a sawhorse, lumber. A table set for two. A daisy in a small vase. A salad and a bottle of olive oil. Brutus is wearing tight-fitting pants and boots, a white shirt. Wanda enters wearing jeans and a T-shirt and carrying her own glass of wine. The music segues into heavy truck sounds. Brutus shuts the window. The outside noise stops abruptly. A socially tense atmosphere.

BRUTUS: When I moved here, this area was a wasteland. Actually, it still is. But now it has pretensions. I tore out all the closets years ago. I like to see my belongings around me. I move my bed almost every day. This table was over by the window this morning. I have everything on wheels. *(Moves a side table a couple of feet during the next line, does that smoothing gesture)* I'm addicted to a feeling of impermanence.

WANDA: Restless.

BRUTUS: Yes.

WANDA: That's so funny.

BRUTUS: How so?

WANDA: I'm the opposite. I've had all this impermanence and all I dream of is of settling down and having a home. What a great space!

BRUTUS: You've got to be kidding.

WANDA: No. It has a romantic pentimento.

BRUTUS: It's a rathole. Precious to me, yes. Though make me a better offer and I'd vacate like a shot. But I don't see that happening. No. This is it. This is the last stop. Awful.

WANDA: Wouldn't you like to have something green?

BRUTUS: Then I'd have to water it. I don't want to take that on. Danke schoen for the daisy.

WANDA: You're welcome. It's become very swank, this part of town.

BRUTUS: I know. Who would've guessed that saying you live in the Meat District would be appealing?

WANDA: No, there's something about it.

BRUTUS: You come up against yourself here. To that much I can attest.

WANDA: You get morose, don't you?

BRUTUS: I brood.

WANDA: This salad is wonderful!

BRUTUS: It's the olive oil. I have very good olive oil.

WANDA: Where do you get it?

BRUTUS: My parents. See? Chiappa. The family business.

WANDA: You have olive groves?

(He gets up abruptly with his dish. Puts it on the side table.)

BRUTUS: I don't. It's an old story. Family's wealthy, I'm not.

(He snatches her plate, though she's still eating, puts it on the side table, and rolls the lot to an offstage kitchen.)

WANDA: But you must do well with your writing.

BRUTUS *(Off)*: I'm broke. I used to make money. I have a body of work. But royalties peter away if there's nothing new to excite the public. *(Reenters)* And there's the problem. I can't write anything new. *(Heads for the open shutter)*

WANDA: What about that idea you were telling me?

BRUTUS: I can't write it. I'll think it, but I can't write it down.

WANDA: Why not?

BRUTUS *(Looking out the window)*: I stare out the window when I should be working. I can't tear my eyes away from the spectacle of the world passing me by.

WANDA: What do you think about when you're doing that?

BRUTUS: My parents. What they want me to do.

(He shuts the shutter. He gestures that he doesn't want to continue in this vein.)

WANDA: Speaking of the past, do you want to hear something really weird?

BRUTUS: Sure.

WANDA: My grandfather lived here.

BRUTUS: What do you mean?

WANDA: I was talking to my Aunt Zelda this morning. She saw your address. This was the first place my grandfather lived in this country.

BRUTUS: Coincidence. The refuge of the unimaginative conversationalist!

WANDA: Why do you do that?

(He's uncomfortable. He gets up.)

BRUTUS: So you were married?

WANDA: Yes.

BRUTUS: Were you in love?

WANDA: I thought so.

(He grabs up some used silverware off the table, exits to the off-stage kitchen, leaving her alone.)

BRUTUS *(Off)*: But it wasn't true?

WANDA: It was a catastrophe. I bought into my husband's lifestyle. I was willing to sacrifice everything that made me *me* to make it a success with him. But the more I gave up of myself, the worse it got. In the end, I was just helping him hate me. If it wasn't for this old boyfriend who sort of rode in at the last minute, I would've been toast. I guess I have boundary issues.

(Brutus reappears suddenly.)

BRUTUS: Who doesn't? After a certain point, select phrases should be banished from the public discourse. I nominate "boundary issues" for inclusion on the list.

WANDA: It describes a problem in contemporary relations.

BRUTUS: Just remember, in order to have boundaries, you've got to have territory!

WANDA: Good point.

BRUTUS: Identity.

WANDA: Yours seems fixed enough.

BRUTUS: I have several identities. There's the me when I'm alone. There's the me that exists in reaction to you.

WANDA: Me? What do I have to do with it?

BRUTUS: You are not me. You are other people.

WANDA: What other people?

BRUTUS: The other Face.

WANDA: You're getting obscure.

BRUTUS: When I encounter a person, have an encounter, it's like looking in the mirror and seeing, instead of myself, a stranger. That's my problem. I've never learned how to hear the voice of God while listening to the words of men. The difficulty of maintaining my original soul. The danger of other people. For instance. I can't pray while someone's looking at me not believing. I'm susceptible to doubt.

WANDA: So you pray.

BRUTUS: Don't you?

WANDA: Yes. I'm not devout the way my grandparents were, but I say a prayer now and then.

BRUTUS: My father's faith is unshakable. He visited me here once. He knelt in that spot and put his head . . . *(Crooks his head in a ritual manner)* Made his devotion. Right here. And I knew God could hear him. I memorized the moment. After he left, I began to pray in that exact pose. In hopes God would mistake me for my father. That's his hatbox. I keep it there. We all have our little rituals. Have your coffee.

WANDA: You're very honest.

BRUTUS: I haven't got an honest bone in my body. I despise honesty. Indirection, that's my modus.

WANDA: I think you underrate yourself.

BRUTUS: Do you? On what evidence?

WANDA: Well, you didn't like my work, you were rude, you blew me off, but then you turn around, you relent, and you have the moral courage to call me, extend an invitation to give it another shot.

BRUTUS: Let's face it. I was horrible the last time we talked.

WANDA: I have to tell you, I got in a cab and cried all the way home.

BRUTUS: I'm sorry.

WANDA: I'm too sensitive.

BRUTUS: How can you be too sensitive? It's like a scalpel being too sharp, a woman being too beautiful.

(Wanda, flustered, giggles. Gets up.)

WANDA: All my roommates say I'm too sensitive.

BRUTUS: How many roommates do you have?

WANDA: At the moment, just one. But I'm always moving. The room-mate thing is just . . . I have that, you know, typically American story. I have a family, but everybody lives somewhere else and there's no . . . village, you know? Someday I'm going to have my own place. That's my dream. I decorate it in my head. I was thinking about everything you said the other afternoon. You really are brilliant at just *riffing*.

BRUTUS: Oh, but everything I say is response. Where's the action? Where's the vision? I can never wrestle myself free of context and give birth to something new. That's why I need isolation. I'm so easily contaminated by the pack. I need an idea that starts in the Present and goes into the Future. But all I do is defend and adjust and curse and worship what's already happened. I can't capitalize on Today. I can't grasp the Now. But it's worse even than that. Because I can't hold on to the Past, either. I've broken with everything. I'm in the soup.

WANDA: You have such an unusual tone. You're very definite, but everything you say seems to hint at something arcane.

BRUTUS: Maybe I know something that I can't say. It's like the story of the fish. Do you know the story of the fish?

WANDA: I don't think so.

BRUTUS: Once there was a young fish named Brutus in the middle of all the other young fish. And they went everywhere together. Well, of course they did. It was a school. So. One day, this bunch of little fish had congregated by a dock and they were arguing about . . . Well, it doesn't matter what they were arguing about. Because they shut up when they heard, up above, people! And they could hear little bits of what these people up above were saying. They kept mentioning "water." Our little school of fish was mystified. What was water? So Brutus said, "I don't know what water is, but I'm going to find out." And he set off. He left the school. Solo. Headed to the open sea. Years went by. Everyone forgot him. But then at last he returned. He was old now. Rusting hooks with bits of line trailed from his jaw. He moved slow, with a certain reluctant majesty. One of the oldest fish recognized him: "Is it you, Brutus? After all these years!" "Yes," he said. "It is me." "And did you find out, did you ever find out, what water is?" "Yes," he answered wearily. "Yes, I know what water is." "Well, since it's been the work of your whole life and we should all very much like to know, please tell us. What is water?" Brutus looked at them, one after the other, his old school, and shook his head. "You'd never believe me," he said. And then he swam away into the gloom.

WANDA: That's the end?

BRUTUS: Yes.

WANDA: It's sad.

BRUTUS: It is sad.

WANDA: Are you a sad man?

BRUTUS: I am more aggrieved than sad.

WANDA: The point of the story almost seems to be that knowledge alienates.

BRUTUS: Once you name a thing, nothing is ever the same.

WANDA: You named the fish after yourself. Your name's Brutus.

BRUTUS: Unless I'm named after the fish. The story's older than me.

(He goes to a cabinet, pours a shot of whiskey.)

WANDA: How old are you?

BRUTUS: Old enough that my parents might outlive me. *(Downs the drink)*

WANDA: Are you all right?

BRUTUS: Why would I be?!

WANDA: I'm so sorry. I didn't mean to offend.

BRUTUS: My fourth wife said "I'm sorry" all the time. You say you're sorry too much.

WANDA: I know. *(The steel shows through a moment)* Someday I'm going to stop apologizing, then watch out. *(Pause)* You've been married four times?

BRUTUS: Getting married repeatedly is like going to college. You learn a lot and the tuition just keeps going up. *(Heads off to the kitchen again)*

WANDA: I watched the movie.

BRUTUS: *Frankenstein?*

WANDA: *The Perils of Pauline*. It's awful. Ridiculous.

BRUTUS *(Off)*: In what way?

WANDA: Well, it's unbelievable. Just one trumped-up situation after another.

(He reenters.)

BRUTUS: You didn't identify with it?

WANDA: No!

BRUTUS: You can't understand the film unless you identify.

WANDA: Did you?

BRUTUS: Very much.

WANDA: Really?

BRUTUS: This is the pickle with your writing. You don't identify with your characters.

WANDA: But I absolutely deeply do!

BRUTUS: No.

WANDA: I worked on that book for sixteen months!

BRUTUS: They've been working on Sixth Avenue for twenty years. That doesn't make it a masterpiece.

WANDA: I am my characters.

BRUTUS: You bear no resemblance. Your characters are heroic cartoons.

WANDA: The movie was without merit.

BRUTUS: Obviously, you didn't understand the movie. Well, how could you? Pauline had curly blond hair. You don't know what that's like.

WANDA: You're not serious.

BRUTUS: I'm perfectly serious.

WANDA: Well, you don't have curly blond hair. Did you identify with her?

BRUTUS: Yes.

WANDA: How?

BRUTUS: I put on a wig.

WANDA: You did not!

BRUTUS: I put on a wig.

WANDA: You put on a curly blond wig and watched the movie?

BRUTUS: Yes.

WANDA: I don't believe you.

BRUTUS: You want to see?

WANDA: Yes, I do!

BRUTUS: All right.

(He reaches into the cabinet and pulls out a curly blond wig on a styrofoam head.)

See? Here it is.

WANDA: You do have a wig!

BRUTUS: I told you.

WANDA: You had that on your head?

BRUTUS: Yes. *(Puts the wig on)* See?

WANDA: You watched the movie like that?

BRUTUS: So I could identify, yes.

WANDA: That's nuts.

BRUTUS: I do what I have to do. If I have to wear a wig, I wear a wig.

WANDA: And it really changed how you reacted to the character of Pauline?

BRUTUS: Of course. Completely. It makes you feel different to have curly blond ringlets.

WANDA: I wouldn't know.

(He takes it off and offers it to her.)

BRUTUS: Put it on, look in the mirror, you'll feel differently. Go on.

WANDA: All right.

(She puts on the wig, looks in the mirror of the wardrobe.)

BRUTUS: You're seeing somebody else now, right? It's not exactly you. You could pass for another person. Maybe even to yourself. You could pass. If you invest deeply enough.

WANDA: Do you seriously think my reaction to *The Perils of Pauline* would be different if I watched it in this wig?

BRUTUS: The wig's only a step, a gesture. It's just a hairpiece. We're trying to fool *you*. You're not so easily going to mistake yourself for Pauline. She did not identify with others. Her power came from the mirror.

WANDA: How do you mean?

BRUTUS: Pauline saw a world that contained only people like her. Reflections that wanted what she wanted, believed what she believed. Her peril and her strength was the same: She was ignorant of everything but Pauline. But you'd have to be more of a waif, wear a little waif dress.

WANDA: I suppose you wore something like that.

BRUTUS: That's right. I did. And here it is. Voilà.

(He pulls out a white waif dress.)

WANDA: You wore a dress? You wore that dress?

BRUTUS: I did.

WANDA: It's very hard to take you seriously knowing that.

BRUTUS: It takes courage to be the right kind of fool. Put it on.

WANDA: What?

BRUTUS: Put the dress on.

WANDA: I will not!

BRUTUS: Come on. You're already wearing the wig. Think of what I was willing to do! I'm a man. You're a woman. It's much less for you to do it.

WANDA: For what I know you got off on wearing it!

BRUTUS: Just what I thought. You're totally unwilling to try on other points of view. That's why you stink as a writer. What are you afraid of?

WANDA: I'd have to take my pants off.

BRUTUS: Oh, come on! You're ridiculous! Just throw it on over your precious jeans.

WANDA: But why?

BRUTUS: The fact that you find it so threatening should be reason enough! You're obviously afraid, entrenched, unimaginative, and bourgeois. You wanna know why your writing doesn't penetrate? Because it's just gutless. Words cost nothing. You need to risk something. You need to put your money down. I risked something to comprehend a woman's pain because

I want to know! That's intellectual passion. That's what sepa-
rates an artist from a woman sponge-painting her bathroom!

(She snatches the dress from him.)

WANDA: Oh, all right, stop browbeating me! If your book hadn't con-
vinced me that you were on to something exciting, there's no
way in hell I would be doing this!
BRUTUS: Admit it. You're doing it because you want to. You're making a choice.

*(She assesses putting the dress on over the jeans and rejects the
idea.)*

WANDA: This isn't going to work. Give me a minute. Stay out of the
kitchen.
BRUTUS: Take your time.

*(She exits. He takes a drink of wine, sings a bit of a folk song,
finishes the glass. She laughs.)*

What?
WANDA *(Off)*: Never mind. Where'd you get this thing?
BRUTUS: Thrift shop.
WANDA *(Off)*: It scratches.
BRUTUS: It's Egyptian cotton.
WANDA *(Off)*: Those cotton-picking Egyptians.

(He sings a bit more. Drinks her wine.)

BRUTUS: You need help?
WANDA *(Off)*: No!
BRUTUS: Too bad.
WANDA *(Off)*: Very funny.

(She reenters in the dress and wig.)

How do I look?

BRUTUS: Like a little moth.

WANDA: Where's that mirror?

BRUTUS: Very good. The mirror's the key to the whole thing.

(He presents her to herself in a mirror.)

Shazam. *(He starts away)* So you're looking . . . *(He goes to the wardrobe)*

(She likes something about the way she looks.)

WANDA: Damn it. Jesus. I *do* look like somebody else.

(He pulls out a little hat from the wardrobe.)

BRUTUS: There's a hat.

WANDA: A hat. All right. Give me the hat. I might as well shoot the moon. *(Puts on the hat)*

BRUTUS: Now look in the mirror. Do you want to see her face? Do you want to see Pauline?

WANDA: Sure.

BRUTUS: You're going to have to be a lot more willing if you want to see something in yourself that you've never admitted before. Now do you want to see Pauline?

WANDA: Yes. Yes, I do.

BRUTUS: Do you contain goodness?

WANDA: Yes.

BRUTUS: And you contain evil. Look in there and forget me. Forget everything else. Look in that mirror and see there the whole world. Everything's there. Everything that's good, everything that's bad. That's true, isn't it?

WANDA: I guess it is.

BRUTUS: It's true. Now concentrate. This is a moral exercise. Look at what in you has value. Everything that has value. Everything worth defending, everything good. Look at that part of yourself, see that part of yourself, let everything else fall away, and say: "I am good."

WANDA: I am good.

BRUTUS: Keep looking in the mirror. "I am good."

WANDA: I am good.

BRUTUS: And you are. Look at that face. You can trust yourself, can't you? You know the best of yourself. Show that, like a shining shield, love that. Ignore the rest and trust that.

WANDA: Okay. Okay.

BRUTUS: Very good. That's Pauline. You're Pauline. Your father left you a ranch. It's your birthright and it's all you have in the world. If I were to ask you, Pauline, under the threat of violence, for the deed to that ranch, what would you say? Give me the deed to your ranch.

WANDA: No.

BRUTUS: Hand over the deed to your father's ranch!

WANDA: I won't do it!

BRUTUS: I'm giving you one last chance to give over that deed!

WANDA: Never! Do you hear me! Though it should cost my life, you slobbering pig! You'll never get my poor dead dear father's ranch! This land is mine! *(Drops it)* Wow!

BRUTUS: How was that?

WANDA: I feel kind of free.

BRUTUS: You've just realized you don't have to be you.

WANDA: But it was me!

BRUTUS: But it was you. Very good.

WANDA: I've never felt so in the right!

BRUTUS: That's it.

WANDA: Oh my God, I'd love to have a picture of this.

BRUTUS: You want a picture, I can take a picture.

WANDA: Really?

BRUTUS: No problem. I'm an excellent photographer. Actually, I do videos now, too. Would you like a video or a picture?

WANDA: A picture I think.

BRUTUS: I took the pictures in *Understanding Japanese*.

WANDA: You did?

(He gets a camera from the wardrobe.)

BRUTUS: Every one.

WANDA: They were very well composed.

BRUTUS: Sit in the chair. No, better! The ladder! *(He pulls the ladder over)* See? It's like the railroad tracks.

(She sits on the ladder, poses.)

WANDA: Like this?
BRUTUS: Try up one rung.
WANDA: Good?
BRUTUS: Good. So far. Now do you want the full experience?
WANDA: What would that be?
BRUTUS: In other words, a pose. Like Pauline would pose.
WANDA: How would she pose?
BRUTUS: Tied up.

(He pulls out a heavy rope. She hops off the ladder.)

WANDA: No way.
BRUTUS: What is your problem? *I'm* not going to tie you up! Just you. Fake it. Lay the rope around your wrists. The camera can't tell the difference.

(He tosses her a bunch of rope.)

WANDA: Oh. Okay.

(She returns to her perch, holds the rope against her.)

Sure. Something like that? How's that look?
BRUTUS: Fine. Now I need to see more violated trust. "Renounce your birthright!"
WANDA: No!
BRUTUS: "Denounce your patrimony!"
WANDA: No!
BRUTUS: Good! Now I'm going to put a glamorous light on you.
WANDA: Make me look good!
BRUTUS: Absolutely!

(He pulls the old movie studio light into place while singing a snatch of some romantic ditty. He turns the light on, then looks through the camera.)

But now the rope's wrong.
WANDA: What's wrong with it?
BRUTUS: It's slack. It's obvious that it's not . . .

(He abandons his post at the camera impatiently and comes over to her. He works on the rope for a second.)

WANDA: Did I move it? Is that better?
BRUTUS: Not like that! Jesus! Here. Just make it believable. A couple of hitches or something. It can't be loose. It's got to be tight, tight, tight. Be brave. That should do it. Let's look at that.

(He goes back to look through the camera. She tries the rope, can't get free.)

WANDA: Where's the knot? I can't reach the knot.
BRUTUS: No? I'll undo it in a minute. This looks much better.
WANDA: Undo it now.

(He heads hurriedly to the cabinet, grabs something.)

BRUTUS: Absolutely! Just lemme just fix the background so the backlight is softer and . . . *press.* OPEN!

(He presses her jaw forcefully. It's painful.)

WANDA: Ow!

(Her mouth pops open. He puts a ball gag in her mouth, pulls the band over her head. She tries to scream. It's quite a muffled sound.)

BRUTUS: And that's as loud as you get, my dear. Not that anybody would hear you on this godforsaken avenue. Not that the hoi polloi would care if they did hear.

(He ties her legs in such a way that they are spread wide.)

There's the East Side, there's the West Side, and then there's the Meat District, where everything's a candidate for dinner. You send me your selfish book. Your fantasy of an ideal world with you in the middle serving tea. I read every page. Do you know what I was looking for? Me. And guess what? I wasn't there. Shame on you. Fortunately, you're not the only one who dreams. And my fancies are more expansive than yours. Because in my perfect world, you show up. True, you're in a pickle. You're helpless. You're humiliated. You have no voice. But whose fault is that? Is there a greater provocation than to be ignored? I don't think so, but no matter. I've got you now. In *my* dream. You don't want me in your club? Fine. You shut me out, I'll shut you down. *(Sings)* What a day for a daydream. *(Drops it)* But daydreams are fiction and fiction is dead, right? So let's set it up. Let's make it real. Why did you send me that book? Didn't you learn anything from your first go-round? Why are you here? Why did you step towards death again? Did you think I was going to jump for joy at your wonderful idea of a world without *me*? Or was this what you were trolling for? Maybe you recognize all of this. The ropes, the feeling, the fear. Did you enlist me to do this for you, you pixie? Did you seek me out to do this for you? When we met, I was playing chess alone. It's hard to play both parts, isn't it? It can be done, but it's hard to be both the Villain and the Victim, and experience the *full* understanding.

(He has been adjusting his clothing, changing into the Villain. He puts on protective goggles. Now he reaches into the cabinet and pulls out a circular saw.)

So you don't get it? You can't identify with Pauline? A woman tied to the railroad tracks, a train coming towards her. The ringlets. The frock! It's absurd, right? Contrived.

(He starts up the circular saw. It roars to life. She's trying to scream, tears running down her face. He cuts a two-by-four in half.)

WELL, HONEY, YOU WILL IDENTIFY WITH PAULINE!
YOU HEAR ME!!! IF YOU EVER GET TO WATCH THAT
MOVIE AGAIN, TRUST ME, TRUST ME, YOU WILL BE ON
THE EDGE OF YOUR SEAT!!!

*(He turns toward her with the saw, heads for her belly. She
screams, screams. Blackout.*

*The headlight of the train—the old movie studio light—bears
down on us. The roaring sound of a train builds, the whistle
screaming. Then, sudden silence.)*

Scene 3

*"Moonlight Sonata" begins to play. The old movie studio light burns
dimly. Brutus enters the darkened room with a candelabra of lit candles.
Wanda has fainted. A second, shorter ladder has been set up near the first.
Wanda revives.*

BRUTUS: Hello? Hi. You fainted. The "Moonlight Sonata." So now
you know something. Now you've had an experience. Something concrete. You're in the soup. You've been living in your
head too long. Don't you feel better?

*(She looks at her stomach, realizes he didn't cut her. She whim-
pers with relief.)*

No, I didn't cut you up. Actually, *we've* had an experience.
That's right. Now there's a *we*. We have a relationship. There's
a bond. Maybe I'll give you a nickname. Any suggestions?
Good idea. Nipples. Let's just put some clips on those. One.
And two. *(Puts clips on her nipples)* Two of the three points of
the triangle. I wonder how the third point is doing? The Delta.
(Climbs the second ladder) But back to Pauline. She's tied to
the tracks. *She's* not gagged. What do you think she really says
to the Villain once she sees the train in the distance? The danger jacking up each moment. At first, certainly, she appeals to
his humanity, his decency. But when that falls flat, she

undoubtedly speaks to him as a Man. She offers herself to him. Of course she doesn't mean it! She's just trying to save herself. But as the approaching train's vibration starts to rage like a hyena through her body, and the concept that this guy is her only hope solidifies into certainty, doesn't it seem likely that her pretense of lust would terrify down into lust itself? That the fiction of her civilized character would start to fall apart? That she would begin, in the savage grip of self-interest, to genuinely experience a ravenous desperate desire to please this man, to indulge this man, if only he will save her? She makes promises. Terrible, beautiful promises . . . And while she says these things, her voice, competing with the train, rises in intensity, in sincerity, in depth of conviction. Until, finally, she breaks through. And she offers to die for him. She loves him. She loves him so much. She is so utterly committed to his will. She is content to die for him beneath the wheels of the oncoming train. All she asks is a single kiss. And at that moment of perfect subjugation, the Villain unties her and drags her limp body off the tracks, and fucks her. He fucks her even as the train roars by like madness. He takes her with such vulturine bloodlust that for a moment the past does not exist. There's only the Now. And her white dress in ruins. He upchucks obscenities, gushes fluids, voids rages, floods her womb, marks her psyche, soils, begrimes everything that could be said to *be* her. Until she's done to the brim. Full. And he's empty. And then he's finished. His clutch loosens, his eyes glaze, his body becomes indifferent. He stands, pulls up his pants, wipes himself off on the tail of his shirt, and starts walking home. As if you'd never existed. You look after him. You make your way to your feet. And. You. Follow him. *(Pause. With a remote, he shuts off the "Sonata")* And here we are. You and me. In reality. I tell you this tale. You can't speak. Your legs are spread. You listen to this story of the girl on the train tracks. And so many things pass through your mind to say to me, some scornful, some pleading, some accommodating. But you are enjoined through circumstance to remain silent. Your inner journey's mysterious conclusion unknown even to you. Because a process endured without benefit of civilized response leads to an outcome beyond the imagination of thought. *(He takes the gag out of her mouth, dabs her lips with a handkerchief)* Let me take this out. What do you want me to do, Wanda? How do you want me to treat you now?

(A sledgehammer hits the door from outside once, twice. At the third blow, the door falls down. Dust rises. A slim, handsome cowboy, Frank, is standing there with a sledgehammer, which he casts aside. He surfs down on the fallen door and draws his gun.)

FRANK: Hold it right there, mister!

BRUTUS: Who are you? Don't shoot! I'm unarmed! I'm an unarmed man!

(Frank throws a massive breaker switch by the door. A photoflash comes out of the breaker, then all the lights in the loft bang up very bright.)

FRANK: Stand away from that goddamn girl!

(Brutus blinks at the brightness. Frank strides over to Wanda and unties her.)

Are you okay, Wanda?

WANDA: Frank?

(She's in shock. She pulls off the nipple clips and throws them down.)

BRUTUS: You know her?

FRANK: That's right. She's a friend of mine.

WANDA: How did you find me, Frank?

FRANK: Your Aunt Zelda had a bad feeling. Gave me the address.

BRUTUS: I think you should go before I call the police. As you can see, Wanda is fine.

FRANK: She is not fine, asshole! She's in shock. What the hell's the matter with you?! What the hell did you do to her?

(Wanda puts her hands on Frank's chest.)

You okay?

(She pushes him away.)

WANDA: Fuck off, Frank. Mind your own business. I'm a big girl now and I'll handle this my own way. You understand English, Frank?! GET OUT and leave us to it!

FRANK: But he's . . . he . . .

WANDA: It's not like before. I'll deal with this . . . one. In my own way. I can handle it. Get out.

(Frank takes a step toward the doorway, hesitates.)

FRANK: Are you sure?

BRUTUS: Don't feel bad, Frank. It's modern life. Either you're the Villain or the Victim. Those are the only roles available. No one is exempt.

WANDA: One favor. Leave me the gun.

FRANK: All right. Good enough. *(Hands her the gun)* Hasta luego.

(Frank exits.)

BRUTUS: Now where were we?

WANDA: First of all, I don't want you to call me Nipples.

BRUTUS: All right. What do you want me to call you?

(She lifts the gun. She takes on a new wildness, a new nobility.)

WANDA: Call. Me. Israel.

(Blackout.)

Act Two

Scene 1

Music: "Watermelon Man" plays again. The cowboy, Frank, sits at a bar tossing cards into his hat. He's gained a lot of weight. Watson, the bartender, a Cockney, looks on. It's the same guy who played Lawrence; he raises a sign that says: NONFICTION. *The music fades, replaced by Frank singing. Watson sweeps up.*

FRANK:
Camptown races sing this song

WATSON:
Do dah! Do dah!

FRANK:
Camptown race is way too long

WATSON:
Oh da do dah day!

FRANK:
Goin' to run all night

WATSON: Right.

FRANK:

Goin' to run all day

WATSON: True.

FRANK:

Bet my money on a bobtailed nag

WATSON: Ouch.

FRANK:

Somebody bet on the gray.

WATSON: Tragic, isn't it?

FRANK: No customers. Not a single goddamn customer. What happened to the drinking public?

WATSON: Take it easy. Why would there be any customers, Frank? It's Sunday morning and we're closed.

FRANK: Maybe we should open?

WATSON: The law says no serving of alcoholic beverages on Sunday morning. It's to promote churchgoing I believe.

FRANK: Church. You go?

WATSON: Not for years. You?

FRANK: Sometimes, but I have trouble with it.

WATSON: Doubt?

FRANK: No, envy. I don't wanna worship, I wanna preach.

WATSON: It's my impression that religions were organized *against* God. Like labor unions.

FRANK: Labor unions! Are you trying to get my goat?!

WATSON: Not a bit.

FRANK: Are you trying to get health benefits?!

WATSON: No, no! I have a perfectly nice little first-aid kit!

(Watson flees behind the bar. Frank starts as if he's heard something. Impasse.)

FRANK: Can't you feel it?

WATSON: What?

FRANK: The silence.

WATSON: Maybe you should *(Knocks on bar)* let it in?

FRANK: I don't think so, kemosabe. I prefer noise and toys.

(Frank pulls out a pack of cigarettes and slams them on the bar.)

Try this on.

WATSON: What's this?

FRANK: Pack a cigarettes.

WATSON: What good's that do me? I don't smoke.

FRANK: Maybe you could start.

WATSON: Why?

FRANK: Try one on the house.

WATSON: Why would I do that?

FRANK: You might like it.

WATSON: Bloody hell, so much the worse. I get addicted. Do you smoke?

FRANK: I quit. That shit'll kill ya.

WATSON: I don't want the cigarettes.

FRANK *(Snatching the pack back)*: All right, so don't have one.

WATSON: Well, you don't have to be like that about it.

FRANK: Oh, I don't, huh?

WATSON: It's just that they make me cough.

FRANK: You begrudge me makin' a livin'?

WATSON: You do all right.

FRANK: So everybody thinks.

WATSON: What's the matter?

FRANK: What do you care?

WATSON: You don't seem to be your jolly self.

FRANK: You ever feel like the old tricks aren't working?

WATSON: I was born feeling that way.

FRANK: Like a monkey on a chain dancing for apathetic children.

WATSON: Poor little monkey.

FRANK: I'm suffering, Watson.

WATSON: From what?

FRANK: Well. In a few words. I'm a very social person and I feel isolated.

WATSON: Okay. I see. So you're down.

FRANK: Exactly! I'm down, Watson. I'm as down as I've ever been, and I hate it. I prefer to be happy. Well, what the hell is that? Who doesn't want to be happy?

WATSON: Lots of people.

FRANK: Really? Why?

WATSON: Otherwise engaged.

FRANK: And then there's my weight.

WATSON: You look fine.

FRANK: I'm fat. Wherever I go, I'm the fattest person in the room.

WATSON: A few pounds is all.

FRANK: I used to be as slinky as a puma. It's all part of the depression.

WATSON: Is that why you took to drugs?

FRANK: Why do you go right to that? I've cleaned up. Been through the Program three and a half times. *(Pops a pill)*

WATSON: What's that you just took?

FRANK: Psychopharmaceutical.

WATSON: What's it do?

FRANK: Do I look like an M.D.? Goddammit, you've gotta have some faith, Watson! How 'bout a slice a lemon?

(Watson goes off for lemon.)

This atmosphere of cynicism is killing me! It's not just you. It's the attitude on every park bench. Look at me. I got something better to offer, but the problem is: It seems like nobody wants it.

(Watson reenters with lemon.)

WATSON: You mean cigarettes?

FRANK: No! I'm talkin' about something intangible and fine. I'm talkin' about my heart. I'm talkin' about my soul. You know what I'm talking about? I'm talkin' about my philosophy.

WATSON: I didn't even know you had a philosophy.

FRANK: How do you think I became a success? It's because I operate from a philosophy.

WATSON: Well, what is it?

FRANK: Me. My philosophy is me. I believe I'm the best so that's what I sell. My message is simple: Be like me. Do like I do. And it works. I'm an idea, I put that idea out there, and people like the idea. The only problem is: People don't like me. They like the idea of me, they try to do like I do, but when they come face to face with the original article, their smile goes crocodile. The upshot? Well, take a gander. I'm alone. Success, yes. But what friends I have are bought and paid for. Nobody just likes me.

WATSON: What about your cronies?

FRANK: A man wearies of cronies.

WATSON: Well, I like you. Lots of people like you.

FRANK: I don't feel it.

WATSON: You want love.

FRANK: That's it. I want love, and nobody loves me.

WATSON: Can't help you there.

FRANK: Why not?

WATSON: It's not that I don't admire you, Frank. I do. I'd like to be you. I'd like to be sitting where you are, and you going about serving me.

FRANK: Well, that's how it was when I was a kid, remember? I used to sweep up and you'd be reading the paper.

WATSON: Those were the days. I thought they'd never end. Why did they end?

FRANK: I remember why. It's the day I made that cup a tea, and you charged me twice.

WATSON: I didn't charge you twice. Up until that point, I'd been giving us both the company discount. That day I decided to retain the discount for management, and abolish the discount for labor. You took it all wrong.

FRANK: It was unfair.

WATSON: Haven't you ever done anything unfair?

FRANK: Not that I like to remember.

WATSON: You overreacted.

FRANK: I by God stood up and took my place at table. I love you, Watson, but you're a son of a bitch when you've got the whip.

WATSON: Who isn't?

FRANK: Me.

WATSON: Hubris. First step on the slippery slope.

FRANK: You're right and I hear ya. That's why it's so good having you
around.

WATSON: The voice of experience.

FRANK: Why, I can look at your face and see every mistake I might
ever make.

WATSON: That's me. I'm a cautionary tale.

FRANK: You're a tonic is what you are! Just lookin' at the second-
rate state you're in gives me a boost!

WATSON: We have a bond.

FRANK: That's right! Goddammit, we do have a bond! We have a special relationship.

(Frank pulls out a pistol, hands it to Watson.)

Here. What do you think a that shootin' stick? It's a beauty,
ain't it?

WATSON: I can't afford to buy any more guns from you, Frank. I still
owe you for the car.

FRANK: You love that car though, don't ya?

WATSON: It is a treat.

FRANK: Just feel the action.

WATSON: Why, when you're anxious, do you always resort to the
sales pitch?

FRANK: Careful now. My daddy always said: "Guns are like Irish-
men. Assume they're loaded."

(Watson has a good laugh.)

WATSON: Ah, I do love a joke at the expense of the Irish. It is a nice
little gun. Take it back. *(Puts the gun down)*

FRANK: You don't have to pay me anytime soon. Shit, you don't have
to pay me at all. Not in money anyways.

WATSON: Then how?

FRANK: I don't know. Wash my back sometime.

WATSON: I can't make up my mind about you.

FRANK: How so?

WATSON: Faust or the devil?

(Frank puts the gun in Watson's hand.)

FRANK: Either way, we're in business.
     (Indicating gun) Man, you look good with that iron Marl-
     boro in your hand. You look like me. Wyatt Earp always said:
     "When you reach for a weapon and it ain't there, it's too late."

WATSON: Did Wyatt Earp really say that?

FRANK: Who cares? He's dead. Why don't you put that little piece a
     punctuation where you can reach it, if and when, so's you don't
     get caught short.

WATSON: All right. Better safe than sorry I suppose.

(Watson stows the pistol under the bar.)

FRANK: That's the way. Deal done. Nothin's quite got the snap of a
     good transaction. What do you think? You want me to stand
     you to a drink? C'mon, I'll buy you a drink.

*(Frank is about to pour a shot. Watson blocks the glass with his
palm.)*

WATSON: I can't have a drink. I'd lose me job.

FRANK: Right. I did make that rule, and it is a good rule. But if
     I don't buy you a drink, maybe you'll start to hate me.

WATSON: You're so insecure.

FRANK: Wouldn't you be? No roots. Born in an orphanage. Every-
     body's child, nobody's son. That's my birth scar.

WATSON: What do you give a damn what other people think of you?

FRANK: What do they think of me?

WATSON: Who?

FRANK: Well, like your buddies.

WATSON: Oh, they think you're all right.

FRANK: No, they don't! *(Pause)* Just all right, huh?

WATSON: Well, the Frenchman, he's never going to get on with you.

FRANK: Louie? Why not?

WATSON: He thinks you're gauche.

FRANK: Gauche.

WATSON: Go on. Ask me what it means.

FRANK: I don't care what it means.

WATSON: It means you're an awkward, embarrassing, clumsy person.

FRANK: Oh I am, huh? You know that an amphibian wants to eat like me, dress like me, and drive an SUV! And when the hell's he gonna give up speakin' French anyway?

WATSON: It's his language.

FRANK: It's pretentious. You don't speak in French.

WATSON: That's true.

FRANK: But you oughta lose that accent. You can if you put your mind to it. Practice speakin' like me.

WATSON: Take my advice. Don't bother about Louie. He's just jealous. There's nothing you can do about that.

FRANK: But I want him to like me!

WATSON: Why?

FRANK: I don't know. I wanna shine. That's the way I am. I wanna shine. So maybe I try too hard. Try to win everybody over. Try and try. But then I gotta tell you, this other thing kicks in, and I get full-up disgusted. Hate everybody. I think: Fuck 'em all. Who needs 'em? I go to my apartment, shut the door. Keep to myself. And cook. That's my passion.

WATSON: I didn't know that. You're a cook?

FRANK: I have to cook 'cause I love to eat. You know what the key to cooking is? Ingredients.

WATSON: Do you know what the problem with eating is: The more you eat, the more you want to eat.

FRANK: I give up cigarettes. I'm off the drugs. I gotta have something.

WATSON: When are you going to sit down with yourself and address your restless soul?

FRANK: Never. Sometimes I have a moment when this silence wraps itself around me like an anaconda. And I feel the hate out there. I look up to the sky for comfort and see the majority is darkness and cold, and that the stars are ignorant and do not care. And that, that's when I have a major chowdown. And as I eat my way to that latest plateau of satiety, the loneliness fades to gold. It's a new day. And I begin to fantasize about what the world *could* be. Don't you sometimes wish we could all sit down and bare our souls and get to some kind of deeper understanding?

WATSON: No.

FRANK: You don't?

WATSON: No.

FRANK: But how could you not want that, Watson?

WATSON: Well, to begin with, it would ruin the poker game.

FRANK: I don't even like poker.

WATSON: You can't kid me. You invented poker. There's that woman again.

FRANK: Who?

WATSON: There's this woman been looking in the window the last few days, but she never comes in.

FRANK: Jesus.

WATSON: What?

FRANK: I know her. Have you ever had a woman where you didn't know where to put her in your head? Where there's a chemistry so intense you can't afford to fuck her and you'd die if you cut her loose?

WATSON: I kind of feel that way about the queen.

FRANK: She is like a queen this one, a queen in trouble, like some Cleopatra. But she's also something altogether new. A new kind of monarch brought to flower in the blood-soaked garden of world guilt. She's a dream, a folktale, her existence justified by prophecies and firepower. A thousand rivers from a hundred countries feed the headwaters of her soul. She's inevitable, impossible, the embodiment of Justice done. I'm telling you, the gods themselves fall back in fear that the hand of man has occasionally forged such a one as this. For when you make an ideal real, the blood will spill like adolescent tears. Is there anything more dangerous than a dream literally realized? Is there anything more . . . romantic?

(Music: The theme from Exodus *with sweeping orchestral arrangement. Wanda makes a big entrance. She's no longer dressed like a graduate student. Now she's in a graceful gown*

*and sunglasses. Frank gets up, takes off his hat, dances with
Wanda. The music stops and they stop with it.)*

WANDA: Hi.

(Frank shoves her away, acting like a spurned lover.)

FRANK: What do you want?

WANDA: I just thought we might catch up. Can I get a beer?

WATSON: We're closed.

FRANK: Watson, serve her up.

WATSON: All right then. *(Serves her)* Happy New Year. I'll be in the
basement putting down poison for the squeakies. *(He exits)*

WANDA: How long's it been?

FRANK: Since when?

WANDA: How long have we known each other?

FRANK: Your whole life.

WANDA: Not that long.

FRANK: Round it off. Your whole life and we have yet to settle a goddamn thing.

WANDA: Time flies. How you doing?

FRANK: Terrific. Business is booming. Ain't sellin' the smokes like
I did, but everybody loves the guns.

WANDA: You always had the knack. Good for you. You put on a couple of pounds.

FRANK: I know. I'm fat.

WANDA: I didn't say that.

FRANK *(Tapping his shirt pocket)*: It's a side effect.

WANDA: Of what?

(She pulls a vial of pills out of his pocket, chucks it.)

What do you need that shit for?

FRANK: When you've been singing up-tempo as long as me, sometimes you need a little help.

WANDA: You're better than that.

FRANK: I guess better ain't good enough. Congratulations on the book.

WANDA: Thanks.

FRANK: Never gave up.

WANDA: Paid off.

FRANK: Bestseller?

WANDA: No. Lotta people hate it. But a loyal following.

FRANK: How's the household side a life?

WANDA: Nothing much.

FRANK: Fibber McGee.

WANDA: All right. I just don't know how to start.

FRANK: Why not start at the leave-off? I untied you, gave you a gun.
You had the drop on that creep. When I left, you were hooked
up like Marge in Charge. How'd it play out?

WANDA: I was rude to you.

FRANK: Doesn't bother me. I wrote you off.

WANDA: No, you didn't.

FRANK: I should have.

WANDA: I was asserting myself. I wanted to stand on my own. You
want me to stand on my own, don't you?

FRANK: I don't know. I admire independence, but I like bein' needed.
So what happened?

WANDA: I got to the point, I thought I could work it out with him.

FRANK: Well, good for you. I like that. Optimism.

WANDA: I couldn't.

FRANK: Don't beat yourself up. Let me tell you something. At the end
of the day, Yes will triumph over No. So how's it shakin' down?

WANDA: A no-holds-barred, twenty-four-car, domestic train wreck.

FRANK: Damn. Well then, maybe you should leave.

WANDA: Where would I go?

FRANK: Good point. It's tight out there.

WANDA: He should leave.

FRANK: Isn't it his place?

WANDA: It was, but now it's ours. And actually, I have a prior claim.
(Pulls a piece of paper out of her garter) My grandfather lived
there long before this guy.

FRANK: He did?

WANDA: And the wording of my grandfather's lease suggests I have
rights. I love the apartment. It's the first real home I've had in
a very long time. But I'm not going to lie to you. I'm in trouble. I'm going to lose it unless I get some kind of help.

FRANK: You mean money?

WANDA: I mean more than money.

FRANK: So you mean money.

WANDA: I'm talking about something more.

FRANK: Somebody's cashing the checks I send.

WANDA: And I thank you. But I need something more.

FRANK: You're losing me. More than money? What are we talking about?

(Watson enters with a case of Coke.)

WANDA: I need Justice.

WATSON: And you came to Frank?

FRANK: What's that supposed to mean?

WATSON: Just popped out. *(Ducks out of sight behind the bar)*

WANDA: Look. I'm a proud person. I put myself through college. I work two jobs. I try to make my own way. But I'm having to defend myself against somebody who's just got nothing else to do. This guy's been unemployed for like a century. His life's a disaster and he's decided to blame me.

FRANK: What's he at?

(The unseen Watson puts four six-packs of Coke on the bar, one after the other.)

WANDA: It's not just him. He has this intense family. And they all have trust funds and grudges the size of Norway. They have blood feuds with the dry cleaner, these guys.

FRANK: I know his family.

(Watson pops up.)

WATSON: The Chiappas. They're tougher than Turkish taffy.

FRANK: They are a little testy.

(Watson disappears again.)

WANDA: Well, the thing is, they all hate me. They got this deadbeat relative and they blame me. They think I'm the problem. And they're willing to pay any amount of money to harass me and get me to move out. I have nobody I can go to. Except you. Everybody hates me except you.

FRANK: Why's everybody hate you?

WANDA: I have no idea. It's just been a historic fact. I must stand for something that I don't even know about. Look, it's a natural thing to want to be independent. Since the day I was born I've depended on you. I'd like that to end. But I need you.

FRANK: And you hate me for it!

WANDA: I don't hate you.

FRANK: No?

WANDA: No.

FRANK: Goddammit, why do I care!

WANDA: You have to care, Frank. It's the only thing that saves you from being a monster.

FRANK: I'm fightin' to keep my hands off you.

WANDA: I feel things, too.

FRANK: But it's always mixed up with money.

WANDA: Are you calling me a whore?

FRANK: If I was poor, would you even talk to me?

WANDA: What do you think?

FRANK: I don't know. I don't want to get involved again. Everything's messy with you. I like to keep things simple.

(Watson pops up from behind the bar, grabbing a pack of soda.)

WATSON: Some people think you're stupid. *(Disappears again)*

FRANK: Well, if I'm stupid, how come I'm doing better than everybody else?

(Watson reappears to grab more soda. Stays up this time.)

WATSON: Some people say it's because you're very lucky.

FRANK: I believe you make your own luck.

WATSON: The people on top always do.

FRANK: And the people on the bottom always talk shit. I wonder how well you'd treat me, Watson, if you were in my shoes. I remember the way it was. I remember what kind of boss you were. I would never treat a man the way you treated me. *(To Wanda)* He charged me twice for a cup a tea!

WATSON: Blimey, I'm sorry about the bloody tea! You're like an elephant! I apologize, I was strapped. I needed cash.

FRANK: It was unjust.

WATSON: Haven't you ever done anything unjust?

FRANK: Not that I like to remember.

WATSON: If I had another shot at things, I'm sure I'd do better.

FRANK: I'm not.

WATSON: I've become understanding of the underdog.

FRANK: That's because you are the underdog!

WATSON: I'd like to think I've learned a bit since the sun set on my supermarket.

FRANK: The only thing that made you compassionate was comeuppance.

WATSON: No, I mean it, Frank! Look at me. I'm sincere. I've changed.

FRANK: Have you?

WATSON: Yes.

FRANK: I swear to God I want to believe you, buddy. You're the closest thing to a father I never had.

WATSON: You know I think of you as a son.

FRANK: When we squabble, it eats me up. We're a family. Families should be able to work things out.

WATSON: It's about trust now.

FRANK: That's right. You've gotta trust me.

WATSON: No, you've got to trust me.

FRANK: Me first.

WATSON: All right. I'm willing to make the gesture. Listen. If you decide you want to help this woman, I'm in. Anything you need.

FRANK: Are you serious?

WATSON: Deadly serious. All my resources. At your disposal.

FRANK: Now are you saying that because I'm a good customer, and your boss, and you owe me money for the gun, or are you saying that because we're friends.

WATSON: Because we're friends, of course.

FRANK: Well, I'm moved, Watson. I'm deeply moved.

(They embrace.)

WANDA: So you'll help me?

(Frank shoves Watson away, finished with him. Watson goes behind the bar; unseen by Frank, he pours himself a shot and knocks it back.)

FRANK: I didn't say that. I'm just seeing how things line up. You got that grandfather lease with you?

(She pulls out a piece of paper and hands it to him.)

WANDA: Yeah. Take a look. I've got a tidy little case there.
FRANK *(Looking it over)*: You're telling me the claim is legitimate?
WANDA: My people were there first.
FRANK: Good! I like that. That's strong. Plain. If you can't say it in ten seconds, what's the point? Tell me something, princess. Smart as you are, pretty as you are, how come I'm the only person who likes you?
WANDA: How should I know? I've always tried to get along. But people have this weird reaction to me.
WATSON: I can understand that. You seem kind of, I don't know, up to something. Shifty. What's your game?
WANDA: You see? This is exactly what I'm talking about. This.
WATSON: You can't fool me, ladylove. You're in on something. There's some kind of plot or conspiracy, an international secret cabala protocol. I'm a bit of a scholar, you know. I read pamphlets.
WANDA: Don't I have a right to an apartment?
FRANK: Well, let's say you're correct. Let's say you do have a claim. Obviously, he has one, too. He lives there.
WANDA: I'm not telling him to move.
FRANK: You're not?
WANDA: No.
FRANK: Oh. Okay.
WANDA: But there is the question of stuff.
FRANK: What stuff?
WANDA: He has stuff and I have stuff, but I have more stuff and nicer stuff than he has so I think that I should have more of the apartment than he does.

FRANK: Well, that's just crazy.

WANDA: No, it's not.

FRANK: Yes, it is.

WATSON: I agree with Frank.

WANDA: Suckass.

FRANK: Did you make a smart remark?

WANDA: Of course not.

WATSON: Yes, you did. And it hurt. Ow.

FRANK: Please be careful with Watson's feelings. We have a special relationship.

WANDA: I apologize.

(Watson puts out his hands to Frank with a gooey look in his eyes.)

WATSON: Hands?

(Frank takes Watson's hands.)

FRANK: Hands across the water, buddy.

WATSON: You know I love you, man.

FRANK: Back at ya. *(Through with him)* Gimme some peanuts.

WANDA: So you'll help me?

FRANK: Well, there is a sticking point.

WANDA: What?

FRANK: Oil. The Chiappa family makes my favorite olive oil.

WANDA: Well, what's more important? I mean, I don't want to exaggerate, but I could be killed. These people are ruthless. I live in fear.

FRANK: I know you have a problem, but this is some rum-tum-yummy olive oil. I've cooked with butter, I've cooked with Crisco. But I gotta tell you, once I tried Chiappa's olive oil, there was no goin' back.

WANDA: So Brutus was right. You're not a hero.

FRANK: You're a little quick to disenchant. Motivations notwithstanding, a man does a heroic thing, why isn't he a hero?

WANDA: Because he gets something out of it.

FRANK: And is that a problem?

WANDA: You want the man to untie the woman from the railroad tracks because it's the right thing to do, not because he's going to benefit.

FRANK: If I untie a woman from the tracks, I'd like to think I'd get a little kiss, if not a good twenty-four-hour fuck session. Otherwise, why get up in the morning?

WANDA: So you won't help me?

FRANK: I didn't say that. I'm going to try to find a way to help you *and* have my salad the way I like it. Can a check solve this? Can I write you both a smart little check?

WANDA: I told you. Just money isn't going to work.

FRANK: Why not?

WANDA: I hate his fucking guts and he wants me dead.

FRANK: How about I give you both a whole shitload a guns?

WANDA: No.

FRANK: Dammit. So what's gotta happen?

WANDA: Dominate us. Tell us what to do.

WATSON: So Frank would be kind of a sexual dungeon master or something? You are a naughty girl. Watch out, Frank. Deep waters.

FRANK: Watson's right. Why me? Why would I get involved in something so unwholesome? Why would I do that?

WANDA: Because you love me.

FRANK: No.

(He starts to walk away, resisting her. She lifts her hand. Their sweeping orchestral Exodus *theme plays; it stops him. The music continues.)*

WANDA: Most people just take up where their parents left off, Frank. Most people just look at their shoes. But you and me, we're pioneers. We lift our eyes and look out ahead. We rejected the tyranny of the Past and fell in love with the freedom of the Future. Out of the rough stuff of Injustice, we resolved to make Practical an ideal. We were dealt with unfairly. Yes. But it made us dream of a better way of life, a place where we would no longer be persecuted. You fought to make a place like that for yourself. I'm fighting for that place now. We call that place Home.

(Frank turns to her, takes her in an embrace.)

FRANK: Goddammit, you can play me like a jukebox! I'm with you, baby.

(The music ends.)

Lemme give you somethin', I wanna give you somethin'. Lemme give you a tank!

WANDA: No! You're a madman!

(Frank pulls out a big, remote-controlled toy tank and presents it to her.)

FRANK: Here, factory fresh. This is primo. You're gonna love it! It's all-terrain!

WANDA: Wow. Thank you, Frank.

WATSON: I've got three. They're great!

FRANK: Try it! Hit the switch!

(She sends the tank whizzing around the bar floor.)

WANDA: Oh, I love this thing!

FRANK: I knew you would. It's got a big motor.

WANDA: Like you.

FRANK: Hush up with that.

WANDA: Can I count on your help with the apartment?

(Music: The theme from The Magnificent Seven *or some other big Western movie starts to play. Frank considers; Wanda hopes; Frank takes her hands, then pulls her to him, committed—all to the music. Watson sets about closing up.)*

FRANK: Let's go straighten this double-dealing cocksucker out. Close up shop, Watson. I'm callin' in my chits. This is a sticky ball a rice and I may need chopsticks.

WATSON: Just as you say.

FRANK: Let's ride!

> *(Frank mounts an imaginary horse, Wanda gets on behind him, and Watson jumps on last. The horse whinnies three times as they rear to the left, to the right, and then straight back. The Western music continues. Frank does a "Yeehaa!" and they ride off. Pause. Wanda reenters, still with the music, and retrieves her tank, which she holds aloft in glory. Then she puts it down, operates the remote, and drives it off. The music segues into the sound of a real tank as she exits and . . .)*

Scene 2

Moody music with an Arabian flavor plays. Brutus is carrying his father's hatbox. He puts it down, and takes out and dons an Arab headdress. Then he rolls the old movie studio light into place and turns it on. He sets up a little video camera on its stand. He takes his place before the camera.

BRUTUS: Take number seventeen: "The Good-bye Video." *(He gets into character)* How long can a man live off good memories? How long before he needs something new? The time is now. I want to say . . . to my father . . . when you see this, I am already dead. You never appreciated my scholarship. I know that. You called me a girl for reading books. Well, I'm not reading books anymore. I am a man of action now. Perhaps you will raise your opinion of me. To my mother: You are no doubt shedding fat tears of sorrow and regret and counting the insurance money you've collected. For the many times you did not love me, for valuing my death more than my life, I want to say to you: I am in Paradise. I am surrounded by virgins and candy and raisins and God is here with me and He doesn't like you very much. But I am not angry anymore. I speak to you from a place beyond anger. I am free. To my wider family, I want to say look at me, how terrific it is to be me, and why don't you all just hope to be as brave and good as I am.

And good-bye. And cut. *(Drops character)* And fuck you for making me destroy myself.

(The lights cross-fade to the sounds of English backbenchers booing. Brutus remains in shadow, his head lowered. The lights come up on Watson talking into a microphone to his constituents, the audience.)

WATSON: Please. Please! My countrymen! I know, I know! I know the question that's on all of your minds. I say it right out: Why do I always side with Frank? Nobody else sides with Frank except when it suits them. Frank sends them money, they take the money, they abuse him anyway. So why am I always shoulder to shoulder with the bloke? The answer is, I do it for you. If I stand next to Frank, if I court the strong and bully the weak, if I walk when he walks, judge when he judges, kill when he kills, if I talk morality and act in self-interest *long enough*, one day I will eat Frank and I will burp and then I will be Frank. And you, my brethren, will be able to reclaim your paramount position in the community. Is it difficult to blend completely with a man so unlike meself? Yes. But I have discovered that many of his movements come quite naturally to me. Many of his actions are not foreign to me at all.

FRANK'S VOICE: Hey you! Hey! Over here!

(From the shadow Brutus directs the movie studio light to pick out Frank in the aisle. Frank appears in a tux, bow tie undone, with a mike of his own.)

FRANK: And I'd just like to say . . .

(He starts singing "You Light Up My Life" or "Take It to the Limit" or some such thing. He joins Watson onstage. Watson sings with Frank now, making it a duet. The sound of a record scratching interrupts them, followed by a hard-rock instrumental. They start dancing. Blackout.
Another record scratch takes us into . . .)

Scene 3

Frantic French rock and roll. Something like "Ça Plane Pour Moi" by Plastic Bertrand. An image in the darkness: a spot up on the devil dancing. The light goes out. Spot on Wanda, in the doorway of Brutus's loft. She dances like a military go-go goddess demanding tribute. She's wearing a red beret, camouflage pants, a holstered gun and a tank top. She gestures, conjuring Brutus's entrance; he's in his Arab headdress. He throws open each of the three sets of shutters in turn. Each time he does this, there is a flash of light and an explosion, from which he staggers back. He reaches Wanda and mock-spanks her in a rage, while she acts mock-shocked. Then he runs downstage, making to speak, but the music grabs him, and he dances across the stage against his will. He crouches facing upstage. Frank and Watson come on with palms in pots, dancing. They set them down, then exit. Brutus rushes to each of the plants and makes rebuking gestures. Then he goes to Wanda, who's still undulating. He becomes mesmerized by her movements until she puts a foot on his shoulder and shoves him down. He scuttles away and climbs a ladder to sit on top of a pile of his possessions heaped in a corner. Frank and Watson reenter with more palms, dancing. They put these down also. Then Frank climbs a centrally placed ladder, and Watson stands upstage holding a club. Wanda throws the big breaker switch. There is a photoflash and the loft is flooded with natural and electric light. We see that Brutus's stuff has been shoved into one corner, and Brutus glowers on top of the clutter. Wanda's side looks great. It's decorated with several green palm trees. Frank sits on top of a stepladder at the dividing line between Wanda's stuff and Brutus's stuff. He's still wearing his tuxedo shirt, minus the tie, and over that, a safari jacket. Watson, in sunglasses, a Castro hat, khaki pants and an orange shirt, leans against the wall with his club in hand.

FRANK: So here we are.

WATSON: All present.

WANDA: Yowsa.

BRUTUS: Yes, here we are! You know. You know. I was just thinking about something. I was just thinking about my childhood.

(Music: The theme from Lawrence of Arabia*)* To be exact, I wasn't exactly thinking about my childhood, which was shit. I was thinking about my heritage. Which I saw in a movie once. The desert! An endless palace of sky. My domain. Riding my camel into infinity. Yip, yip! Night comes. We make camp. We talk in the great tent about philosophy, mathematics. The hypnotic flames of the campfire blackening and illuminating our eyes. Spontaneously, we compose poetry of great insight and organic beauty. That's what you can never understand. You can never understand what I have lost. You can never understand what it is to be . . . *(Leaps to the floor as the main musical theme explodes)* A Jew German!

(He takes a triumphal walk around the space. Gives Watson a disrespectful gesture. Then he pulls his headdress taut. The music ends abruptly. He does a little dance, chanting:)

> The sand is soft
> Don't need no mattress
> I'm a nomad
> I got no address!

(Wanda gently removes Brutus's headdress, crosses to his hat-box, and puts it away.)

WANDA: You know what your problem is, Brutus? You have a tendency to believe your own publicity. When I got here, this place was godawful. Now it's green. I see a spot that needs a plant. Bear with me now. Doesn't that look great?

BRUTUS: Do you see what she's doing? She put that plant right in the middle of what's left of my half of the apartment!

FRANK: Wanda, can you speak to that?

WANDA: It's just temporary. A little buffer until we work things out.

BRUTUS: And when would that be? You keep saying that and you keep pushing my stuff in the corner.

FRANK: Well, that's where I come in, Brutus. I'm here to help you and her to come to an understanding.

WATSON: But you're going to consult me, right?

FRANK: Absolutely, Watson. You got the big stick?

WATSON *(Raps it twice on the wall)*: Right here.

FRANK: Good man. I'm sure we won't need it. So what do you all want?

BRUTUS: I'll tell you exactly what I want. I want her out.

FRANK: Not gonna happen.

BRUTUS: Why not?

FRANK: Not fair to Wanda.

BRUTUS: What about me?

FRANK: You've gotta be reasonable.

BRUTUS: It's my apartment, I want her out. That's reasonable.

WATSON: Wanda needs a place to live.

BRUTUS: So what? I need a place to live. This is it. I don't like these plants. I don't like any of this. I want my stuff where it used to be.

WANDA: You mean, all over the place. Well, that's not going to happen. You lost that right when you attacked me.

BRUTUS: Who are you to say what rights I have and what rights I don't have?

WANDA: I'm the woman with the gun.

WATSON: Bang, bang.

BRUTUS: What happened to the rule of law?

WANDA: Oh, so now you're Atticus Finch?

FRANK: I'll apply the Law once we hash out what's legal.

BRUTUS: Who's going to decide that?

FRANK: Me.

WATSON: The Law is a living thing.

BRUTUS: Either I should be armed or you should disarm!

(Brutus advances toward Wanda. Watson steps in and whacks Brutus in the stomach with his club.)

WATSON: That's far enough!

(Brutus staggers back to his side of the loft.)

FRANK *(To Watson)*: Stand down.

BRUTUS: I want my stuff spread out nice the way it was!

WANDA: You mean like a slob. Then I wouldn't have anywhere that was clearly mine.

WATSON: That would be confusing.

WANDA: And anyway, I have more stuff and nicer stuff than you.

FRANK: Let's not be judgmental.

BRUTUS: That's because I'm poor.

FRANK: You need a job?

WANDA: I'd be poor, too, if I didn't work.

WATSON: Lazy. We don't like that.

BRUTUS: I can't work under these circumstances.

FRANK: I hear you.

WANDA: You're a bum.

FRANK: That's inflammatory.

WANDA: It's a fact. You used to be somebody, but for the last ten thousand weeks you just read what you've already written.

BRUTUS: That's because I can't function in this living situation.

WANDA: What are you talking about? You weren't working when I got here.

BRUTUS: But I was thinking about it!

WATSON: Sure you were.

WANDA: All you do is talk about the glory days and knock up ignorant girls.

WATSON: Overpopulation.

WANDA: You're a bum!

BRUTUS: Who are you to call me a bum?

WANDA: Who am I? I'm not a bum, that's who I am. I'm a productive member of society.

FRANK: Cheese and crackers.

BRUTUS: How can I be productive when I'm so angry? It's insane what you're doing here. This is my apartment! I was so happy before you came.

WANDA: What are you talking about? You were miserable.

BRUTUS: But I had hope! I had the hope of being happy. Now I have no hope.

WANDA: So hope! Who's stopping you. Hope your brains out for what I care.

BRUTUS: I can't hope in this atmosphere of hostility and aggression. The situation's unbearable. To begin with, the bathroom's on her side.

FRANK: Wanda, that does seem tough.

WANDA: All he has to do is ask.

FRANK: Brutus?

BRUTUS: Well, I have to go now.

WANDA: No problem. Come ahead.

WATSON: Full speed.

> *(Brutus crosses to the bathroom. Wanda draws her gun and blocks the way.)*

WANDA: I just have to check you out. Arms up?

> *(Brutus puts his arms out. She frisks him. He complains to Frank.)*

BRUTUS: This is what I have to go through. This is my life.

WANDA: You brought it on yourself. Drop the pants.

> *(He turns away from her, drops his pants.)*

WATSON: Bloody hell, I'm not here!

WANDA: Spread 'em.

> *(He spreads the cheeks of his ass. She shines a flashlight in his ass. She's satisfied.)*

Okay. Pull 'em up. You can go in.

> *(Brutus exits into the bathroom.)*

FRANK: Jesus Christ, girl. What are you kids doing? This is no way to live.

WANDA: You think I like it? But you don't know this guy. You wouldn't believe the stuff I've found in his ass.

FRANK: It seems to me that this kind of atmosphere can only lead to terrific hostility and misunderstanding.

WANDA: What do you suggest?

WATSON: You know what I think?

FRANK: Hold the thought, Watson. I'm very interested in what you think, but I'm busy right now. *(To Wanda)* For starters, maybe you could give him a little more room. He's gotta get buggy living in that little bit of a corner.

WANDA: You know, I would love to do that. But first, I want him to show that he's changed. I want him to demonstrate that he's capable of being a good roommate.

FRANK: How?

WANDA: I'd like him to suck my foot.

FRANK: Huh? What?

WATSON: What's that?

WANDA: I'd like him to open his mouth very wide, so I can stuff my foot in it, and then I'd like him to suck it.

WATSON: Yucko.

FRANK: Wanda, has it ever occurred to you that what you may be looking for here is Revenge?

WANDA: I'm not interested in Revenge.

FRANK: That's because there's a certain negative history here, that you and Brutus may simply not like each other enough to live in the one apartment?

WANDA: He's free to go.

(Brutus comes out of the bathroom with a detonator in his hand, and wires going into his clothing.)

BRUTUS: I'm not going anywhere. I was here when you got here, and I'll be here when you're gone.

WANDA: Are you wearing explosives?

(Brutus lifts his shirt to reveal dynamite stuffed in his pants.)

BRUTUS: That's right!

(Frank and Watson flee from Brutus.)

FRANK: Whoa, Matilda! Fire in the hole!

WATSON: It's the blitz!

BRUTUS: This is what I have to do to be taken seriously! You all think you can decide my life without me. You are mistaken. My future's mine.

WANDA: Did you flush? *(Exits to the bathroom)*

BRUTUS: I demand exactly half the apartment! No, better. I demand that everything go back to the way it was before she moved in here! No, better yet! I demand that things go back to the way they were before I was born.

WATSON: That isn't the future you're talking about, mate. That's the past.

WANDA *(Off)*: Oh! What a pig! *(The sound of a flush)*
(She comes flying out of the bathroom) Let me lay it out for you. You wanna live with me, you flush.

BRUTUS: I don't want to live with you.

WANDA: Fine. Go back to the old days, call it the future, just do it somewhere else.

BRUTUS: I'm not leaving.

WANDA: Good. Perfect. Then join your dead relatives you love so much, cash your chips, go ahead, hit the detonator.

BRUTUS: You don't fool me.

(He grabs her hand and tries to force her to push the detonator button. She's terrified.)

You don't want to die, do you? Do you? And that's why I'm stronger than you.

WANDA: You don't know me! You don't know me! How 'bout this?

(She grabs the club from Watson, and hits Brutus's arm and then shoulder. Brutus falls down. She hits him three more times while he's on the ground.)

How does this feel, you sadistic bastard!

BRUTUS: Oh my God! Help! She's a criminal!

WANDA: You hate me. You attack me. I fight back. You cry foul.

(Watson steps toward Brutus.)

WATSON: But he didn't attack.

(Wanda forces Watson back with the club.)

WANDA: He's wearing explosives!

BRUTUS: Did you see that? She hit me! Do it again. Where's my camera? Did you see what she did to me?

FRANK: Easy, Wanda.

BRUTUS: You're the sadist!

WANDA: And MY PEOPLE were here before YOU!

FRANK: Hey there, Wanda, that stick's for defense!

WATSON: She's out of control.

(She tosses the club to Watson.)

WANDA: I don't need the stick. I'll beat the shit outta you right now! Come on!

FRANK: What a piece of ass!

WANDA: That's right! *(To Brutus)* You wanna fuck me, Popeye?!

BRUTUS: I'll push this button.

WANDA *(Taunting him, touching her nipples)*: Push my button!

BRUTUS: I've already made my good-bye video. I have the courage.

(Wanda goads him, clucking like a chicken.)

FRANK: Wanda!

BRUTUS: I have the courage!

(Brutus fends them off with the threat of the detonator. Frank and Watson are on one side, and Wanda on the other. Wanda tears the detonator out of his hand when he's distracted, tosses it away, pulls her gun, and forces Brutus back. He climbs up on top of his stuff.)

WANDA: Courage? Courage is a virtue. When you say someone has courage, that's a compliment. We do not compliment people for exploiting social covenants like Freedom and Trust for the purposes of murder!

WATSON: She's tougher than the ghost of Christmas yet to come!

BRUTUS: Freedom.

WANDA: That's right. Freedom. You can't stop it, you can't fight it, it won't be denied.

FRANK: That's right. As a concept, it's a hands-down winner. Free-dom. That's the temple of gold.

BRUTUS: Is it? I've seen nothing to show that Freedom makes you virtuous. You're not virtuous. You're just fat. You applaud your own lack of definition while you stuff your face. You love your fat ass while your soul starves. While children starve. What are you willing to give anybody without looking for something in return? Nothing. And that's why I'm going to prevail over you. Because I value my soul over my flesh. Because I'm willing to die.

WANDA: Nihilistic little git.

WATSON: It takes courage to kill yourself.

WANDA: It takes courage to get up in the morning and do something with your life. It takes courage to have children and educate them. To make things that are of use. It takes courage to live.

WATSON: It takes money, too.

FRANK: Watson.

(Wanda mutters in grief and anxiety.)

WANDA: *Cherchez la femme?* Where has she gone? No more!

FRANK: What's the matter, Wanda?

WANDA: Too late. Nothing. I'm tired. I've been dealing with him for a little too long. I need a break.

(She pulls out her tank and remote.)

I think I'll go for a ride. *(She sets the little tank going across the floor)*

BRUTUS: Where are you going? What are you doing? What is that?

FRANK: That's twenty-five-wheel drive.

WATSON: One hundred yards to the gallon, fully loaded, automatic transmission.

BRUTUS: Stay away from the place where I pray.

WANDA: What do you mean? Your daddy's hatbox?

BRUTUS: Don't. That's where my father made his piety.

WANDA: I'm sure my grandfather prayed there, too.

FRANK: I think Jesus ate dinner there.

WATSON: Lunch it was!

BRUTUS: That's where my father talked to God. It's my only certainty. That's where I try to talk to God.

WANDA: Maybe it's where Abraham talked to God.

BRUTUS: Please. Don't mention Abraham.

WATSON: Abraham.

FRANK: Honest Abe.

BRUTUS: Have some respect for something in my house.

WANDA: I have a thought I'd like to share with you.

(She drives the tank nearer and nearer to the hatbox.)

Abraham is Abraham is Abraham. And this is in my way.

(She suddenly stomps the hatbox, destroying it. With an animal cry of pain, Brutus rushes to the ruined hatbox and picks it up. He takes it to his area.)

BRUTUS: Cruelty. Your idea of Freedom is cruel.

(Wanda pulls a potted plant onto the spot.)

WANDA: Now doesn't that look better?

BRUTUS: Did you see that? Did you see? She doesn't respect anything about my life. She doesn't respect what's important to me. She wants respect. I can't take any more! And I won't. Die!

(Brutus puts down the remains of the hatbox and picks up a knife. He rushes Wanda, trying to stab her. Watson grabs his knife arm, stopping him.)

WATSON: Now! Now! Give it up!

(Frank plucks the knife from Brutus's hand and leads him away.)

FRANK: Come now, Mister Man. Don't get so het up. Look at me. Do I get excited? Be like me. You'll feel better.

BRUTUS: I don't want to be like you!

FRANK: Lemme talk to you. Are you willing to talk?

BRUTUS: I'll talk to anybody who wants to talk. I'm a reasonable man. It's her!

WANDA: Hah!

FRANK *(To Brutus)*: Lemme try something out on you. You seem like a savvy guy. I had some real estate problems early on in my life and I settled 'em pretty good. I see how it is with the apartment here. Seems to me like what you need is a fresh start. A whole new thing. *(Puts his arm around Brutus's shoulder)* How 'bout we put you on a nice big reservation, set you up with a first-class casino?

BRUTUS: What do I look like? Set her up on a reservation. Give her a casino. I'm not leaving this apartment, she is.

WANDA: I have a God-given right to be here.

FRANK: Now let's not drag Jesus into this.

BRUTUS: She wasn't talking about Jesus, you moronic ill-informed nouveau riche pig!

FRANK: Oh that's right. You guys believe in a vengeful God. But hey, we're all children of Abraham, right? That's some story. That's a fork-in-the-road story. God tells Abraham to sacrifice his son Isaac. But at the last minute God said, "Abe, scuttle that idea. Human sacrifice, dammit, we're past that." I believe that was the beginning of the Jesus angle. Drop that eye-for-an-eye thing, move on. You know what? I'd like to think if Adolf Hitler was a Christian, he wouldn't a killed the Jews.

WANDA: Adolf Hitler was a Christian.

FRANK: I'd like to think, if Hitler was born-again, there never woulda been a Pearl Harbor.

WATSON: The Japanese bombed Pearl Harbor.

BRUTUS: They were backed into it by passive-aggressive actions on the part of the United States.

FRANK: Who told you that?

BRUTUS: I read history.

FRANK: Well, you musta had the book upside down there, buddy. The Japanese started World War II all by themselves. And they got their ass kicked.

BRUTUS: The Japanese were manipulated. They were victims.

FRANK: They were goose-steppers on the move.

WATSON: What about Hiroshima?

FRANK: Sometimes I wonder where you're coming from, Watson.

BRUTUS: But what about Hiroshima, Mister Nice Man? How do you explain Hiroshima?

FRANK: It's funny how you guys love to remember Hiroshima, but you get all fuzzy about Pearl Harbor. You ever hear of cause and effect?

BRUTUS: Who put you in charge of history? One man's integrity is another man's sin. You push me into a corner and leave me no civilized response. But I tell you! I will not be the Villain!

WANDA: You should've thought of that before you tied me up and came at me with a power tool!

BRUTUS: And I'd do it again! You know why? Because you're a Nazi!

WANDA: I'm a Nazi? I'm a German Jew!

BRUTUS: And I'm a Jew German!

FRANK: Now maybe you guys could help me here. What's the difference between a German Jew and a Jew German?

BRUTUS: You're not serious.

FRANK: I know I'm a dumbass not to know, but humor me.

WANDA: A Jew German is a German Jew who hates himself!

BRUTUS: No, a Jew German has faith!

WANDA: A German Jew has faith! I don't know what a Jew German has! He believes Mohammed rode to heaven on a white horse!

BRUTUS: She believes the front page of the *New York Times*! Who's crazy?

WANDA: I am a member of the modern world!

BRUTUS: I'll tell you what you are. You are a creature of racial theory. You, the German Jew, were created by Adolf Hitler.

WANDA: Keep Hitler out of this.

BRUTUS: It can't be done. Hitler made you.

WANDA: Don't!

BRUTUS: You're every bigot's fantasy. "Put them on a boat and send them somewhere. Give them their own country."

WANDA: Shut up!

BRUTUS: When you kill me, you kill yourself. When you kill yourself, you kill me.

WANDA: As long as you end up dead.

BRUTUS: Look at yourself in your righteousness. What you've become.

FRANK: Well, you know what the problem is.

BRUTUS: No, tell us.

FRANK: We're all Jews. That's the crux. That's what you have to understand. It's just that some of us is Jews with a twist is all.

WATSON: I'm Church of England.

FRANK: That's a Catholic with a twist. Catholic is a Jew with a twist. See what I'm saying? Muslim? You ever look at the Koran? The Koran is the Bible thrown in a blender. Muslim is a Jew with a twist. Me, I'm born-again. But you know damn well what I was born first time. A Jew. We're all Jew boys here, squabblin' over who's got the best book. *(Points to Wanda)* And this here's Mamma. That's Jew Mamma.

BRUTUS: That's not my mamma.

FRANK: That's Jew Mamma.

BRUTUS: That's not my mamma.

WANDA: If I was your mamma, I'd slap my own face for what I done.

FRANK: All right, all right. People. How we gonna resolve this?

WATSON: Do you want my opinion?

FRANK: Sure, Watson, what is it?

WATSON: Well, I think you should be very cautious, that's all. Exercise restraint. This is a tricky situation and you wouldn't want to get it wrong.

FRANK: Thank you for that illumination. Look. I wanna get home tonight. I tell you what I'll do. I'll pay for a couple of Polacks to come down here and partition this place. That way you can share the apartment and not have to deal with each other. How's that?

BRUTUS: No.

WANDA: No. *(Exits)*

BRUTUS: Give me guns. Give me guns like you give her.

FRANK: No.

BRUTUS: Why not?

FRANK: Because, at your best, what you want doesn't exist. And at your worst, you're a genocidal street-hustling criminal fucker.

BRUTUS: I see I'm going to have to speak your language. What are you gonna do when you get home, Frank? Are you gonna cook? Will you be using any *oil*? My family's kinda horrified at the way Wanda's been treating me.

FRANK: I have always had the greatest respect for your family.

BRUTUS: They'd like to see that reflected in the way you handle my apartment problem.

(Wanda reenters with some beautiful fabric and a candle. She kneels down, puts the fabric on, shawl-fashion, and lights the candle.)

WANDA: You're a thug. That's what this is all about. You're a bum and a thug. I've dealt with thugs before. I tried to get along with them. It doesn't work. And I swore then: Never again.

FRANK: I like your grit, Wanda. But the danger with the showdown mentality is you end up in the middle of Main Street with fatalities.

WATSON: That's never stopped you.

FRANK: Watson there, you are a prickly pear.

WATSON: Sorry.

(Wanda, afflicted with anxiety and grief, mutters and rocks.)

WANDA: *Cherchez la femme?* Where has she gone? No more.

FRANK: What's the matter, Wanda?

WANDA: Too late. You were right, Brutus. Fiction is dead. We see through the story. The fiction of civilization is dead. All that's left is the Beast.

BRUTUS: Are you calling me a Beast?

WANDA: Yes.

WATSON: It's her, Frank. She gives me pause, that's all. Who's to say she's not a little bit deluded? You know, I read a pamphlet a fella gave to me. It explains how there was no Holocaust.

BRUTUS: There's excellent good scholarship and pamphlets and websites that prove there wasn't. No Holocaust. Everything you do, you justify with this Holocaust, and maybe there was no Holocaust.

WANDA: Oh. Wouldn't you like to think so. Because if there was no Holocaust, then I never needed to come here in the first place. If there was no Holocaust, then I am the Holocaust.

BRUTUS: Maybe you are. Maybe you're a cancer! It's not right that you're here.

WANDA: But is it wrong? My friends, I have to be somewhere.

BRUTUS: So do I.

WANDA: I will be somewhere.

BRUTUS: So will I.

WANDA: I'm not going to vanish so that you don't have to feel guilty.

FRANK: Nobody's asking you to vanish.

WANDA: You're not, but they are.

WATSON: Maybe Frank doesn't have all the facts. Maybe if Frank had all the facts, he wouldn't side with you. He'd side with Brutus here.

FRANK: I'm not siding with anybody.

BRUTUS: That's a crock!

WANDA: You raped me. Every chance you got.

BRUTUS: You asked for it!

WANDA: How?

BRUTUS: You moved in here! What did you expect?

WANDA: I have to be somewhere. Does that mean I have to be raped?

BRUTUS: I'd do it again.

(She stands and asks, not without tenderness:)

WANDA: What happened to you? You were a sophisticated man.

(Brutus starts to break down.)

BRUTUS: What good did it do me? I feel as if God cannot hear me. I pray and pray . . .

(Wanda kneels down again.)

WATSON: Maybe God doesn't like what you're doing.

BRUTUS: Shut your fucking mouth! What am I doing? Nothing but fighting back against years of humiliation at the hands of . . . of . . .

WANDA: God.

BRUTUS: No! God loves me.

WANDA: Why? Why would He love you?

BRUTUS: Because I am devout.

WANDA: I'm devout. Isn't God behind everything that happens? If you're unhappy with how life has treated you, isn't your argument with God and not with me?

BRUTUS: I have no quarrel with God.

WANDA: I think you do.

BRUTUS: I am in a fight to the death with a squatter.

WANDA: We're all squatters.

BRUTUS: I live here. I've always lived here.

WANDA: We're all refugees, we're all somebody's idea of scum. If History were about Justice, we'd all be on the street. Nobody's entitled to a home and we all need one.

WATSON: Now wait a minute. That's all well and true here, where there's nothing, but it's different with me. I have a culture. And culture deserves protection.

FRANK: Get off it, boy! Don't get upright on me! You flushed some poor bastards out of their hole to make a place for yourself just like we all did. And you gotta live with that, just like we all do. But I am not going to stand here and allow the crimes of my grandfather, or the arrogance of your grandfather, or the lease of her grandfather, or the humiliation of his grandfather, to stand in the way of a functioning civilization now! And I am by God gonna have that nice olive oil on my salad until I find something better!

BRUTUS: We'll see about that.

FRANK: Yes, sir. We shall.

WATSON: You're a bit selfish, Frank. And I don't feel completely consulted.

FRANK: You had your chance to rule the world, Watson. Did you do any better?

WATSON: No. But I'd like another shot.

BRUTUS: What about me? When do I get my turn?

FRANK: I ain't keeping time to the tappin' toe of no ayatollah.

WATSON: I remember my past with a blushing lust.

WANDA: I remember when the world turned away and I was on fire.

BRUTUS: I will not endure my humiliation in peace! I remember when all of this was mine!

FRANK: I wish the lot of you would get amnesia! What good is History if all it does is drive you mad? What good is History if it's just a story that makes you hate?

WATSON: But but goddammit, man! Goddammit, Frank! If I am in some sense your father. If you are in some sense my son. Listen to me! You have no moral authority as long as you make and sell so many guns! So many guns. *(Pulling guns out of Frank's pockets and throwing them on the floor)* So many guns.

(Watson walks away. Frank just stands there. A long pause.)

FRANK: I don't like to think about that.

WATSON: You're not a simple man. You have to stop behaving as if you were a simple man. As if things were simple.

BRUTUS: No one's talking to me! No one's talking to me! Do you think I am an extension of your imagination? You take what's mine and you give it away. You give away my home. Why should I stand for it? I suffer! I am suffering!

WANDA: You want to know the truth? I know what's happening to you is wrong, and I don't care. You're the same animal that's always been chasing me. Well, I've stopped running, I've stopped dreaming of getting along with you. You can get along with me, you can leave, or you can drop dead. It's up to you.

BRUTUS: And do you think God likes what you're doing? Do you think God likes what you've become?

(Wanda stands up. She puts on her red beret. She turns to steel.)

WANDA: It's my turn.

WATSON: To what?

BRUTUS: I don't have to put up with this.

(Brutus picks up a gun off the floor.)

FRANK: Watch out!

BRUTUS: No more. It ends now. Die!

(Music: The theme from Z or Zorba or some movie like that. Brutus shoots her. The gun is very fake, the gunshot prerecorded. She screams, but does not fall.)

WANDA: OH NO YOU DON'T! NOT THIS TIME!

(She pulls her pistol and shoots him. Same deal. He cries out, but does not fall. They stagger toward each other.)

BRUTUS: I EXIST!
WANDA: I exist.
BRUTUS: GOD IS GREAT!
WANDA: God IS great!
BRUTUS: You ruined my life!
WANDA: If I die, you die!

(Wanda swings in slow motion, roundhousing Brutus. They both cry "Boom!" to simulate the blow. Brutus swings at Wanda. Same deal. Then Wanda chokes Brutus. He makes a choking sound. Brutus reciprocates. Same deal. Suddenly, they start making out, on the verge of fucking. They stop, just as suddenly, look at each other, and double over, making vomiting sounds. Then they stagger away from each other three steps, wipe their mouths, sigh in satisfaction, and look at Frank. Frank shakes his head.)

FRANK: You two are some sick puppies. That was like watching a snake swallow its ass.

(He heads over to the pile of clutter, pulls out a folded-up card table. He brings it down center, and starts snapping open the legs. The others all seem to have expected this, and start pulling up chairs.)

Shit. Anybody for a game of poker? I was hoping it wouldn't come to this, but you know how that goes. Last game I played lasted forty-five years or so. Hate to start another one so soon. Who's in?

(One by one they sit down at the table. One seat downstage is empty.)

WATSON: I'll play. Tanks okay?
FRANK: Fine. Guns good with you?
WATSON: Why not.
WANDA: Deal me in.
BRUTUS: Can't we play chess?
FRANK: No. We got players to accommodate.
BRUTUS: All right.
FRANK: The old familiar faces.
WATSON: What are the stakes?
FRANK: We'll get to that.
BRUTUS: Frank?
FRANK: What?
BRUTUS: Would you mind if I called you something besides Frank?
FRANK: Like what?
BRUTUS: Would you mind if I called you Caesar?
FRANK: All right, you can call me Caesar, Brutus.
BRUTUS: I want to deal.
WANDA: No, me.
FRANK: Don't worry. Everybody's gonna have to deal.
WATSON: What are the stakes?

(Wanda is seized by emotion again, mutters.)

WANDA: *Cherchez la femme?* Where has she gone? No more.
FRANK: What's the matter, Wanda?
WANDA: I'm pregnant. *(They gasp)* Or am I dying?
FRANK: Those are the stakes.
WANDA *(To the audience)*: Come and see us again.
BRUTUS: We're here every night.
WANDA: It's never exactly the same. But we're here.
FRANK: There's a seat here for ya.
BRUTUS: After all, we're playing with your money.
WANDA: And my life.

(Frank starts singing:)

FRANK:

　　Camptown races sing this song

WATSON: I'll take two.

FRANK:

　　Do dah! Do dah!

BRUTUS: Two.

FRANK:

　　Camptown race is way too long

WANDA: One.

FRANK:

　　All the do dah day!

WATSON: Feeling lucky?

FRANK:

　　Goin' to run all night!

WANDA AND BRUTUS: Nah..

FRANK:

　　Goin' to run all day . . .

WATSON: All together.

　　(Frank sings the verse again. And the others come in in a muted and sad way:)

FRANK:

　　Camptown races sing this song

OTHERS:

　　Do dah. Do dah.

FRANK:

    Camptown race is way too long

OTHERS: Yeah.

FRANK:

    All the do dah day

OTHERS:

    Goin' to run all night

FRANK:

    Goin' to run all day

OTHERS:

    I bet my money on the bobtailed nag

FRANK:

    Somebody bet on the gray.

WATSON: Tragic, isn't it?

(The players lay down their cards and hold the pose. The light stays on them a long moment and then fades away.)

END OF PLAY

Where's My Money?

This play is dedicated to Ira Pittelman, for his humanity.

Production History

Where's My Money? was originally produced by the LAByrinth Theater Company (John Ortiz and Philip Seymour Hoffman, Co-Artistic Directors; Jinn S. Kim and David Zayas, Producers; Carla Nakatani and Justin Reinsilber, Associate Producers) in New York City, opening on July 18, 2001. It was directed by John Patrick Shanley; the set design was by Michelle Malavet, the lighting design was by Sarah Sidman, the sound design was by Eric DeArmon, the costume design was by Mimi O'Donnell, the fight choreography was by Blaise Corrigan and the stage manager was Dawn Wagner. The cast was as follows:

SIDNEY	David Deblinger
CELESTE	Yetta Ann Gottesman
HENRY	John Ortiz
MARCIA MARIE	Florencia Lozano
TOMMY (called Hernan this production)	Chris McGarry
NATALIE	Paula Pizzi

Where's My Money? was subsequently produced by the Manhattan Theatre Club (Lynne Meadow, Artistic Director; Barry Grove, Executive Producer) at City Center Stage II in New York City, opening on November 7, 2001, with the same artistic team and the following cast change:

HENRY	Erik Laray Harvey

Characters

Sidney
Celeste
Henry
Marcia Marie
Tommy
Natalie

Place

New York City.

Time

The present.

Set

Two doors, one tall, one short. Furniture as needed.

Prologue

In the dark, the theme music from some whodunit kind of show, like the theme from Perry Mason, *is heard. We see a series of vignettes, coming attractions, underscored by the music. Each character sees or senses something frightening before the lights cut out.*

Lights up on Natalie in a bed, asleep. She starts awake. A nightmare. Lights out on her.

Lights up on Sidney, sitting in a chair reading a book. He lowers the book, starts at the sight of something. Lights out on him.

Now we see Marcia Marie. She's in her kitchen with a broom. She turns around, smiling, sees something awful. Lights out on her.

Henry is discovered, flattened against a wall. The shadow, the hands of someone approaching. Henry cowers in fear.

Blackout.

Scene 1

Lights up on a French coffee café in Soho. We're outside. It's late morning. We see Celeste, a darkly attractive woman with a slightly bohemi-

an feel, talking on a cell phone. She has a low voice. She's excited and alarmed by the call. She sits at a little blue table, with a hot drink and the remains of a muffin. There's a notebook and paper on the table.

CELESTE: Wait! She tied knots in his tie, she shoved the tie up his tushie, and then, at the key moment, she ripped the tie out like she was starting a lawn mower. Pup-pup-pup-pup-PWONK! The last knot was huge. But here's the twisted part. The next day he goes to the office—he's wearing the tie. Other than that, it wasn't a very good movie. What? What's that? I can't. I can't! I'm in a public place. Turquoise. You are? Right now? You mean for real? I'd like to see that.

(Natalie appears. She's about the same age, also attractive, a little harder maybe, more prosperous. She recognizes Celeste and points and waves. Celeste mimes shock and happiness at seeing Natalie.)

Natalie! *(Gestures she needs a minute more on the phone. Into the receiver)* Can you hold a second? Shut up! *(Covers the receiver)* Natalie! How are you? Oh my God!
NATALIE: I'm getting coffee. Should I join you? You have a minute?
CELESTE: Yes! I'll finish up while you're . . .
NATALIE: Great!

(Natalie goes into the café. Celeste resumes her call.)

CELESTE: I gotta go. What about— *(The caller cuts her off)* What's Friday like for you, Friday night? Kenny's got a gig. Okay, I'll be there. That's just my number. Okay. See ya then.

(Celeste puts her cell away. Natalie returns with coffee. Celeste starts to greet her.)

NATALIE: Hey Celeste, whadaya know? It's so great to see you!
CELESTE: You too!
NATALIE: Where did you go?
CELESTE: Where did *you* go? You dropped out of the world! You look great, Natalie. You look really put together.

NATALIE: I sort've am together.

CELESTE: Did I hear you got married?

NATALIE: Two years.

CELESTE: Congratulations!

NATALIE: Thank you. You look so hokie-stokie!

CELESTE: What does that mean?

NATALIE: Sex bomb.

CELESTE: I'll accept that.

NATALIE: Are you still with that guy?

CELESTE: Kenny. Yeah.

NATALIE: In the same place?

CELESTE: Yeah, same place. *The room.* Where are you?

NATALIE: Upper West Side. Two rooms. It was Henry's aunt's when she . . .

CELESTE: What are we doing? Let's sit. I'm set up over here.

NATALIE: Good idea.

(They sit.)

Well. Here we are. The accounting department.

CELESTE: I was secretarial.

NATALIE: Is that a ring on your finger?

CELESTE: I guess so.

NATALIE: I mean it looks like an engagement ring . . .

CELESTE *(Simultaneously)*: An engagement ring.

NATALIE: Well, is it?

CELESTE: That's what Kenny called it.

NATALIE: Well, isn't that what it is then?

CELESTE: He didn't exactly ask me. He just said that's what it was.

NATALIE: A guy says, "Here's an engagement ring," it isn't a big leap to . . .

CELESTE: Yeah, but he put it on *my* Visa card.

NATALIE: Oh. Well that's . . .

CELESTE: Questionable. Yeah.

NATALIE: Are you still acting?

CELESTE: I take classes, but I haven't gotten much work. I have a great coach, but my agent is . . . I'm not even sure I have an agent. I have to get into that. That's the next thing. There's always a next thing.

NATALIE: But I mean . . . did you . . . ?

CELESTE: Did I what?

NATALIE: You know. Get an operation?

CELESTE: No, I never did. I decided against it.

NATALIE: So you still have the limp.

CELESTE: Yeah, but it's not very noticeable.

NATALIE: It was the first thing I registered about you. Here was this sexy young girl, she wants to be an actress, but she has a limp. Can they fix it?

CELESTE: There's nothing really wrong to fix. It's how I'm made. It's just a slight disproportion between my left and right hip. I guess, at a certain point, I decided to accept myself as I am.

NATALIE: So if you're not making money acting, how do you get by?

CELESTE: I temp. I'm a secretarial temp. Just like I always was.

NATALIE: Did I hurt your feelings?

CELESTE: No.

NATALIE: I'm such a rhinoceros.

CELESTE: It's better.

NATALIE: Think so?

CELESTE: At least you tell the truth.

NATALIE: That's what I think, but maybe I'm just an asshole.

CELESTE: Even if you are an asshole—which you're not—at least you don't compound it by pretending to be sensitive.

NATALIE: I did hurt your feelings.

CELESTE: Well, what do you think?

NATALIE: So I did. I thought I did.

CELESTE: You just about said I'll never get a job because I'm a cripple.

NATALIE: An acting job.

CELESTE: Well, I'm an actress!

NATALIE: But you don't work.

CELESTE: Lots of actresses don't work!

NATALIE: And maybe those girls shouldn't be actresses.

CELESTE: You got a mouth on you, you know that? I forgot this characteristic. The truth-teller.

NATALIE: Well, I'm an accountant. Bottom line.

CELESTE: When it suits you.

NATALIE: What's that mean?

CELESTE: Stuff.

NATALIE: Huh?

CELESTE: My white enamel alligator pin.

NATALIE: I don't follow.

CELESTE: You liked it.

NATALIE: What?

CELESTE: When we were working together. I had this white enamel pin. Of an alligator. You liked it, and you did something.

NATALIE: Are we in the same conversation?

CELESTE: I left my jacket over my chair. When I came back from lunch, my white enamel alligator pin was gone.

NATALIE: This is back three years ago?

CELESTE: Yeah.

NATALIE: Are you saying three years ago you thought I took a pin off your jacket while you were at lunch?

CELESTE: It's more like a nagging slight unfounded suspicion I want to definitely put to rest.

NATALIE: There had to be six people in that office, messengers coming and going, the coffee cart. Why would you think it was me?

CELESTE: I don't know.

NATALIE: Did I seem guilty?

CELESTE: No.

NATALIE: Then how did you come to think I took your pin?

CELESTE: No good reason.

NATALIE: But then why did you think it?

CELESTE *(Big confession)*: Because the day before, I took your red beret!

NATALIE: You did?

CELESTE: Yes.

NATALIE: I had a red beret? I guess I did. You took it?

CELESTE: Yes. I've been carrying that confession around for three years. *(She removes the beret from her purse)* Actually, I've been carrying the beret for three years. Here it is back. I'm sorry.

NATALIE: Why would you take this?

CELESTE: Because I'm insane! And then I tried to justify my bad behavior by deciding you took my pin!

NATALIE: But I didn't take your pin!

CELESTE: I know you didn't take it! I wish you had. Then we'd be even. You can just walk away. I'll understand.

NATALIE: Listen. Let's just say we're even, okay? So you took some raggy beret that didn't belong to you. Forgive yourself. We've all done worse.

CELESTE: Thank you.

NATALIE: No big deal.

CELESTE: I'm such a case.

NATALIE: Forget it.

CELESTE: No. You're a nicer person than me.

NATALIE: No I'm not.

CELESTE: Yes, you are. I wanna learn from you. I wanna learn to deal. Maybe I should look at my life without makeup. My life is bad. Well, it's not that bad but . . . I enjoy reading. I don't wanna feel sorry for myself but . . .

NATALIE: Is it Kenny?

CELESTE: He's not helping. But it's him too. I'm not getting work and I'm turning thirty, and I just got this huge bill for the ring . . .

NATALIE: I would've thought you'd already turned thirty?

CELESTE: ALL RIGHT, I've TURNED thirty! So your marriage is good?

NATALIE: I mean, actually, you must be thirty-one.

CELESTE: Yes. All right. I forgot. You *are* an accountant. Thirty-one. I'm glad we got that straightened out. So how's your marriage? Good? Better? Bad?

NATALIE: It's good.

CELESTE: Nice for you. I'm glad. And you have a job you like?

NATALIE: It's solid.

CELESTE: So you see what you're saying? Look at the picture. You've got a life.

NATALIE: Well, I made choices.

CELESTE (*Cries*): No. It's karma. I try to make choices, but nothing sticks. I just float.

NATALIE: How's Kenny doing?

CELESTE: I think Kenny hates me.

NATALIE: He does not!

CELESTE: We've been together for so long, and his life is so not happening, and he is smoking so much dope.

NATALIE: How's the band?

CELESTE: The band broke up. Kenny does weddings now as a pick-up deal. But mostly he just sits in the apartment and looks at me like I'm "The Thing That Ate His Life."

NATALIE: Is he depressed?

CELESTE: He's a lazy, stoned drummer in a cheap Hawaiian shirt. He's like a depressing piece of furniture. What's your husband do?

NATALIE: He's a lawyer.

CELESTE: A lawyer. What happened to that other guy?

NATALIE: Who?

CELESTE: You know who.

NATALIE: Tommy. Well, I knew that wasn't going to work out. That was just sex.

CELESTE: You were nuts about him.

NATALIE: He was a porter. I wasn't going to marry a porter.

CELESTE: Did he ask you?

NATALIE: No.

CELESTE: That was hot. That thing you had with him.

NATALIE: You never saw us.

CELESTE: I remember the way you looked. He was all over the way you looked.

NATALIE: Yeah, well, it was hot.

CELESTE: I feel like running something by you.

NATALIE: What?

CELESTE: Maybe not.

NATALIE: All right.

CELESTE: I'm having an affair.

NATALIE: Oh wow. Who?

CELESTE: Six months now.

NATALIE: Does Kenny know?

CELESTE: He acts like he doesn't but, I mean . . . There's evidence.

NATALIE: Phone calls?

CELESTE: No. Bruises.

NATALIE: So this guy's violent?

CELESTE: *We're* violent. We both have a lot of anger. It's sort've Latin.

NATALIE: He's Latin?

CELESTE: No.

NATALIE: Uh-huh. So you hit him, too?

CELESTE: No. But we're in it together. It must sound bad. It's hard to explain.

NATALIE: Why'd you tell me?

CELESTE: I haven't told anybody.

NATALIE: Then why me?

CELESTE: He slaps me. He spanks me. He makes me crawl around the floor like a dog. He calls me names. And then I go home to Kenny and act like nothing happened.

NATALIE: So Kenny knows.

CELESTE: I don't know. Kenny blows so much weed he may think I'm something on TV.

NATALIE: He must know.

CELESTE: Who knows what Kenny knows? He's English.

NATALIE: And this guy you're having this . . .

CELESTE: He has read the book that God wrote on my flesh. I've always been afraid to say what I want. He knows what I want and he makes me do it. Get this. He gave me a gun.

NATALIE: He what?

CELESTE: Sometimes I'd be headed home late. He was worried about me. So he gave me a little gun. How sexy is that? I know. Sick.

NATALIE: Not necessarily. But what's the deal exactly?

CELESTE: There is no deal. I see him about once every week and a half. He calls me, I show up somewhere, and he burns down my fucking house.

NATALIE: He's married.

CELESTE: Yeah. I don't care.

NATALIE: You care.

CELESTE: You know what I mean.

NATALIE: And you know what I mean.

CELESTE: Let me control the way I tell this story, okay?

NATALIE: Okay.

CELESTE: There's an atmosphere with this guy . . . of murder. He wouldn't murder me—that's not what I'm saying—but it's there. Like an aroma. I could smell this thing on him when we met. He was introducin' himself, sayin' hello, bein' nice. We're in a public place. I remember thinkin', he's going to rape me. And seeing, like, police photographs in my head. Of me. And right like that, right out of that, I gave him my phone number. I walked away like there was a camera recording me and music I was walking to. And I felt like I was in a ghost story about love. A week later, we meet up. I'm alone with him for the first time. It's in his office. I walk in his office. He closes the door. "Click." And I feel this weight come over my arms and legs. I was scared. 'Cause he was goin' to do something to me. And I wanted him to do something to me. I was afraid and I wanted to be afraid. I wanted fear. I was tired of being "good girl." The first time I went to him, I went to his office, I dressed all in white. Can you imagine? Like a sacrifice. I had this book, *Return of the Native*. And I just started talking about Eustacia Vye because I was so nervous. And he didn't call me on it. He didn't say, "Why are you talking about this book? That's not what's going on here." He just talked back to me about Eustacia Vye. But while he talked, he put his hand on the bone in my chest, and he slowly pushed me down. He never stopped talking about what I was talking about, but he was pushing and I was going down. And then his hands and my whole anatomy went to this other world and we did things without words. What we were saying was like we were one bunch of people in one room, but what we were doing was we were another bunch of people in a very different room. A room without words. We had a secret from ourselves. There was a lot of blood. I got my period right in the middle . . . He's . . . He was big. I guess it knocked something loose. He hadda go out to a store and buy me a raincoat to put over myself. 'Cause, Natalie, I looked like I'd just been born. And this was in an office. This was in a man's office. In the middle of the day. Do you know what I'm talking about? You do kinda, don't you?

NATALIE: Celeste.

CELESTE: What?

NATALIE: I don't like this whole freaking thing! What are you doing?

CELESTE: I know.

NATALIE: I don't see you for two years . . .

CELESTE: But you do know what I'm talking about, don't you? In some way?

NATALIE: No.

CELESTE: God, I really thought in some way you would . . . I haven't told anyone. I thought you . . .

NATALIE: You were mistaken.

CELESTE: I guess we never knew each other very well.

NATALIE: No.

CELESTE: But you were more like me . . . before.

NATALIE: Maybe. Maybe I was turned on by dangerous, stupid shit when I was younger.

CELESTE: Okay. I'd appreciate it if you didn't . . . repeat this conversation.

NATALIE: I won't.

CELESTE: But I am a little bummed out that we can't talk. I need to talk to somebody. I can be pretty hard on myself.

NATALIE: I think you're inviting a conversation you don't wanna have.

CELESTE: But I do want to have it. Look, I'm in trouble.

NATALIE: You're in some underworld.

CELESTE: Yes, I am. That's true.

NATALIE: But you wanna see it as positive and I can't help you with that. It's not positive. You've got it wrong.

CELESTE: Then straighten me out.

NATALIE: Are you sure?

CELESTE: Yeah. I'm inviting it. I want a reaction.

NATALIE: All right, I'll just lay it out for you. You're a whore.

CELESTE: What?!

NATALIE: Don't. Please. It's hard enough without you playing surprised. Don't tell me you haven't thought about the fact that you're a whore. A *stupid* whore.

CELESTE: Natalie.

NATALIE: I'll break it down for you. First thing. The count. Let's do the count. You're thirty-one. Next year, you'll be guess what? Twenty-three? No. Thirty-two. And it goes on from there. Older, older, older. A flight of stairs going down, down, down. You're like a quart of milk reaching its expiration date. Have you ever tried to sell a pumpkin the day after Halloween? That's what you are facing. Are you ready? I don't think so. Is it just? Who cares. Pick a fight with God. See where you get. It's the truth of what it is to be a woman.

CELESTE: Not in France.

NATALIE: France! Then go to France! Climb the Eiffel Tower. Feed the pigeons. Maybe they'll be glad to see you. Please! You're in America. Do the math. Next. You've gotta face the facts. You've got a birth defect. You've got a limp. How many parts are there for limping girls?

CELESTE: Laura in *The Glass Menagerie*.

NATALIE *(Simultaneously)*: Laura in *The Glass Menagerie*. And that's it! Have there been any productions of that play?

CELESTE: Yes.

NATALIE: And did you get that part?

CELESTE: No.

NATALIE: Then it's time for you to stop office-temping and doing Romeo's girlfriend in acting class and get a bona fide fucking job. It's two plus two. You have to drop the lollipop and pick up the car keys! Next issue. Kenny. This may sound tough, but I'm going to say it anyway. Kenny's your best bet.

CELESTE: No way!

NATALIE: Yes, he's a loser. But what are you at this point? Maybe together you can pull your car out of the ditch and make some miles down the road. I know where you're at, Celeste. There's a million women like you. You don't want to look at your story 'cause you don't like your story, so you just close your eyes and tell yourself a fucking fairy tale. And you know what that makes you? In a world of men? Totally exploitable. 'Cause you want the lie. You got no interest in the truth. What's the truth ever done for you? The truth of your life is like a bad magazine. Boring story, lousy pictures. Which brings me to your mysterious, exciting, cheeseball stud. Who smacks you around because he's afraid of his wife. Do I even have to talk about this rodent? A married violent scumbug who slips you a Saturday Night Special for what? Valentines Day? You can't look at what this guy pegged the minute he smelled that thrift-shop essential oil you use for perfume. You're a push-over. Is this your notebook?

CELESTE: You don't like my oil?

NATALIE: What have you been writing?

CELESTE: Poetry.

NATALIE: Poetry. You're going down in flames. Unless you get it together, they are going to pass you around like chicken wings.

CELESTE: I can't believe you called me a whore.

NATALIE: Hasn't he called you a whore? Haven't you called yourself a whore?

CELESTE: Never mind what I call myself! We're talking about you.

NATALIE: No, we're talking about you. I'm not the one in trouble. What's your definition of a whore anyway?

CELESTE: I don't know.

NATALIE: A romantic woman. Romance is for men. Women who settle for romance get used.

CELESTE: Where do you get off? What is this conversation?

NATALIE: This is the conversation you wanted.

CELESTE: Well, I'm stopping it!

NATALIE: Suit yourself.

CELESTE: You have no right to call me what you called me.

NATALIE: I have the right.

CELESTE: How do you figure that?

NATALIE: Because I was a whore, too. A sloppy, stupid whore. But then I made a choice.

CELESTE: To what?

NATALIE: Not be. There are two groups of women in the world. You've got a choice to make.

CELESTE: What about following your soul?

NATALIE: What if you have a damned soul? Are you gonna follow it down to the burning shitheaps of hell?

CELESTE: Maybe.

NATALIE: You are ten years old. You don't get it, do you? How about this. I wouldn't even introduce you to my husband. How about that?

CELESTE: Why not?

NATALIE: What if your soul told you to fuck him?

CELESTE: That's ridiculous.

NATALIE: It's not ridiculous. You probably would fuck him.

CELESTE: I would not! What do you think I am?

NATALIE: I already told you what I think you are. And what every woman like me thinks every woman like you would do if she got the chance.

CELESTE: But off what basis do you say such a thing?

NATALIE: You like it to be wrong. To be a secret. A married man is the perfect thing.

CELESTE: You have no romantic feelings!

NATALIE: What I have and what I do are two separate things.

CELESTE: You said you were a whore.

NATALIE: And I was.

CELESTE: So were you with a married man?

NATALIE: No. But it was bad anyway.

CELESTE: How?

NATALIE: He wasn't a serious contestant. He was uneducated, he had a dead-end job, health problems. He was rough with me. My feelings about him were cheap.

CELESTE: Romantic.

NATALIE: Same thing.

CELESTE: Maybe you're the one who needs to be straightened out.

NATALIE: I don't think so.

CELESTE: All right. Look. I know you have a point, but the only thing that makes me get up in the morning is this guy. Everything else is lousy. I have to have something to look forward to.

NATALIE: Give him up. Marry Kenny.

CELESTE: Aren't you afraid to give such big advice? I mean, what if you're wrong?

NATALIE: I'm not wrong.

CELESTE: What if what was right for you isn't right for me? We're very different people.

NATALIE: We're different because I got on with my life, and you didn't.

CELESTE: What if we're more different than that?

NATALIE: Everybody's basically the same. I was you.

CELESTE: I don't believe that.

NATALIE: That's because you're a romantic. There is no one right person for you, Celeste. This isn't about destiny. It's about making decisions with your head instead of your ass.

CELESTE: But what about my needs?

NATALIE: You need a roof over your head. You need an orthopedic surgeon.

CELESTE: I need other things more than that. And if I don't get those things, I don't get being alive.

NATALIE: Enough. Bite the bullet, make the changes.

CELESTE: You're tougher than me.

NATALIE: That's an alibi. But even if it's true, you can get tougher.

CELESTE: I'm frightened to do that.

NATALIE: I thought you liked being frightened?

CELESTE: I don't wanna live an idea instead of a life.

NATALIE: Are you saying that's what I'm doing?

CELESTE: You tell me.

NATALIE: All right, that's exactly what I'm doing. I'm controlling what happens in my life. I'm looking down on my day and moving stuff around till it's right. I'm in control.

CELESTE: I went to a self-actualizing kinesiologist yesterday.

NATALIE: What is that?

CELESTE: Sort of a psychic.

NATALIE: Oh God. That is so perfect.

CELESTE: She told me I was going to see my future today.

NATALIE: Maybe I'm the future you.

CELESTE: I don't want to be you.

NATALIE: Celeste. You're pathetic. Wake up! Would you? It's sad to watch somebody just fuck everything up. I think you need to go home, take a good hard look in the mirror, get real, make choices. You need to take one day and get brutally realistic about the facts of your life. And *do* something about it.

CELESTE: You don't know the things I think about. When I'm alone. It's okay, I know what to do.

(A man, Tommy, appears and approaches their table. Celeste sees him first.)

Hello?

TOMMY: Hello.

(Natalie turns and sees Tommy. She almost faints. Celeste doesn't know what's going on.)

CELESTE: Is there . . . ? Natalie? Natalie?

(But Natalie only stares at Tommy.)

TOMMY: Where's my money? Where's my money, Natalie?

CELESTE: Is he b . . . ? *(To Tommy)* Excuse me. Excuse me? Shoo! Come on! Back to weird world! Schmuck.

(Tommy just walks off slowly.)

Who was that? *(No answer)* Are you okay? Should I . . . I'll get you some water.

(Natalie grabs Celeste as she gets up, stopping her. She's frightened.)

NATALIE: Stay!

CELESTE: What is it? Are you in trouble?

NATALIE: No.

CELESTE: Do you owe that man money?

NATALIE: Yes.

CELESTE: How much do you owe him?

NATALIE: A couple of thousand dollars. Twenty-seven hundred dollars.

CELESTE: And you haven't got it?

NATALIE: You don't understand.

CELESTE: Is he a criminal? Are you . . . *("In danger?")*

NATALIE: He's . . .

CELESTE: 'Cause I could walk you right over to the police station.

NATALIE: That man's been dead for two years.

(Natalie and Celeste look at each other. Blackout. A pronounced wolf howl is heard, then something like Howlin' Wolf singing "I Asked for Water" kicks in as we move to . . .)

Scene 2

A working-class bedroom on the Upper West Side. Music is playing on a boom box: Something like Howlin' Wolf singing "I Asked for Water"; it's pretty loud.

Henry, a twenty-seven-year-old, self-educated, street-smart guy is reading a book in his bathrobe. Natalie is in a brightly colored T-shirt

*and men's boxers. She regards him a moment. Then she starts danc-
ing to the music, seductive. No response from Henry. He looks at her
and goes back to reading. Suddenly, she barks:*

NATALIE: Henry! I'm in the room. Can you deal with the music please?

HENRY *(Hits the button on the player to stop the music)*: Yes, my precious little cohabitator?

NATALIE: How can you read and listen to that voodoo music?

HENRY: I like to do two things at once. I'm like you that way.

NATALIE: What's the book?

HENRY: *Crime and Punishment.*

NATALIE: Why do you like that?

HENRY: Who said I like it?

NATALIE: Why would you read something you don't like?

HENRY: Who said I don't like it?

NATALIE: You're such a fuckin' lawyer.

HENRY: I'm reading about guilt. Not guilt in court. Guilt inside.
Most things never get to court. Most trials go on in the heart.
This is the minutes of a trial conducted in the heart. Sidney
was reading it. He lent it to me.

NATALIE: You wanna be like Sidney.

HENRY: No, I do not. I wanna *be* Sidney. He's a partner. And he didn't
pass the bar the first time.

NATALIE: Neither did you.

HENRY: That's my point. It shows that it doesn't mean shit about
ultimately achieving my desire. Sidney did it. I'll do it. Simple
as that.

NATALIE: You will.

HENRY: That's right. I will. Because I never give up. Even if I should.

NATALIE: I count on that.

HENRY: Yeah. You left the front door open again.

NATALIE: You're such a nudge.

HENRY: And when I went to play my music, there was music in there
I've never heard. You have secret music?

NATALIE: Listen, why don't we get a joint checking account?

HENRY: We've been through that.

NATALIE: I know. Your first wife fucked you over so now you handle
the money.

HENRY: Left me nothin' but a King Tut medal.

NATALIE: But you wear it.

HENRY: What, are you jealous of King Tut?

NATALIE: It's a bit of her.

HENRY: That bug you?

NATALIE: Yeah.

HENRY: You never said.

NATALIE: I said it now.

HENRY: Fair enough. Point taken. *(Removes the medal from his neck and gives it to her)* Here.

NATALIE: Just like that?

HENRY: Just like that. Problem solved. Life as it should be.

NATALIE: All right. Hasta la vista, golden boy. Back to Cairo. *(Tosses the medal)* You the man.

HENRY: Just steppin' up. Give you a role model.

NATALIE: I don't need a role model.

HENRY: You kiddin'?! Have I ever said no to you?

NATALIE: No.

HENRY: You need money?

NATALIE: No.

HENRY: Those my boxers?

NATALIE: Yeah.

HENRY: Fuckin' thief. Why don't they look like that on me?

NATALIE: That's where I come in.

HENRY *(Indicating a pin on the boxer shorts)*: What's that?

NATALIE: Just a pin to hold them up.

HENRY: A little alligator. *(Steps away, examining her)* Is that you?

NATALIE: Very nice.

HENRY: But there's a thing I can't figure for Sidney. His wife. What's that about?

NATALIE: I'm the accountant. I should be the one doing the numbers.

HENRY: History says otherwise. There's a little matter of a two-hundred-dollar fork.

NATALIE: That was handmade, solid silver.

HENRY: Silver costs something like six dollars an ounce. The fork weighed about two ounces. That brings us up to twelve dollars. The other hundred and eighty-eight was for what?

NATALIE: Workmanship.

HENRY: Workmanship my long-suffering ass. How about the one-hundred-and-ten-dollar candle?

NATALIE: That was a very beautiful thing!

HENRY: It was, but then you lit it. And it melted like candles do. You are not going to eat through our savings buying the crazy things you like to buy. Now, I'd like to discuss this book. The issue in this story is how long can this guilty motherfucker live with it? That's the question. Everything else is known. The crime and who did it is known. Everything except the exact weight of hypocrisy a man can't carry. And that question is what makes me turn the page. Who woulda thought that was such an interesting question to me? Life ain't like that, is it?

NATALIE: Like what?

HENRY: Life doesn't have that narrative drive. Life doesn't hook you.

NATALIE: Sometimes it does.

HENRY: No, life is boring. People are boring. Books and movies are fake because fake is better. In books and movies the story syncopates. It finishes with a bang. Life is a siege. Life is an army outside a city that never falls. I have clients come in and tell me their story and it's always the same fuckin' cha-cha. They blame somebody. Everybody comes in and blames the other one. He did this, she did that. Playin' the blame game. People are predictable as Monday after Sunday and boring as a bag lunch.

NATALIE: Am I boring?

HENRY: Absolutely.

NATALIE: Bite me.

HENRY: As a story. What's the big revelation with you? Nothing. You're an ordinary person.

NATALIE: Maybe you're just failing to see how interesting I am?

HENRY: No, I'm not.

NATALIE: Maybe I'm boring to you . . .

HENRY: As a *story*.

NATALIE: . . . 'cause you're boring and your understanding of people is boring.

HENRY: If something interesting were to manifest, trust me pumpkin, I would be goosed. I'm on a vigil for that shit.

NATALIE: No. You keep things boring because that's how you like it.

HENRY: Okay. And how do I do that?

NATALIE: Like with the checking account. You're afraid to be surprised by what I'd do if it was a joint account.

HENRY: You mean I don't want the excitement of getting ripped off?

NATALIE: I wouldn't rip you off.

HENRY: Of course you wouldn't 'cause you can't.

NATALIE: Goddammit, I'm not some hustler trying to get over on you, Henry! I'm your fucking wife!

HENRY: Oh, you're flashin' the credential. The wife.

NATALIE: Damn right I am!

HENRY: So we're gettin' serious.

NATALIE: I am exactly serious. I've been serious.

HENRY: That's grim.

NATALIE: We're married married married. When does the trust kick in? When are you gonna relax with me and take the ride?

HENRY: Why do you want a joint checking account?

NATALIE: So I can write checks.

HENRY: You tell me the check, I'll write it.

NATALIE: I wanna write the check!

HENRY: What check?

NATALIE: No check in particular. If you died, I'd get the money!

HENRY: So you're fantasizing my death.

NATALIE: If we divorce, I'm entitled.

HENRY: Oh, you want a divorce. All right. 70/30 and you're out.

NATALIE: You are so into intimidation.

HENRY: I'm a matrimonial lawyer. That's the job.

NATALIE: You're my husband, that's the job.

HENRY: I don't think that's supposed to be a job.

NATALIE: With me? Are you serious? I'm twenty-five hours a day, eight days a week. I'm the hardest job in— *(He kisses her)* America.

HENRY: That's my job.

NATALIE: I don't want a divorce.

HENRY: Why not?

NATALIE: Too expensive.

HENRY: Sport of kings.

NATALIE: Divorce.

HENRY: You were the first one to use the word.

NATALIE: Take it back.

HENRY: Is that allowed?

NATALIE: Make it up to you.

HENRY: How?

NATALIE: Whatever you want.

HENRY: How 'bout love?

NATALIE: That's what I want, too. I don't want to be married by myself.

HENRY: Me neither.

NATALIE: I know.

HENRY: But how do I get you?

NATALIE: I'm right here.

HENRY: Me, too.

NATALIE: What's in the way?

HENRY: Us.

NATALIE: Henry, let's do it. Tell me what to do.

HENRY: Tell me what you want.

NATALIE: I need you to tell me what to do.

HENRY: What do you want to do?

NATALIE: Just tell me and I'll do it. Anything.

HENRY: What?

NATALIE: Jesus! You're killing the whole thing!

HENRY: Why didn't you tell me?

NATALIE: Why don't you know?

HENRY: Don't bother with me then! I was readin' my book, listenin' to my music!

NATALIE: Sucking your fucking thumb.

HENRY: That shitass attitude.

NATALIE: It's just the truth.

HENRY: Then I don't want the truth.

NATALIE: Then talk to somebody else.

HENRY: No! You! I'm talkin' to you. You think you're smarter than me.

NATALIE: No, I don't, Henry.

HENRY: Well, you're not! "I can do the checkin' account!" If you're so smart, why don't you have a checkin' account I wanna be joint with? Huh? I'll tell you why. 'Cause I'm the thing that makes this marriage work. Not you!

NATALIE: Okay.

HENRY: I've always been the thing! That's why you married me. Because I could make it happen for you. You would've just . . .

had no life without me. No stability. I give you the check when you need the check. You can depend on that. It's boring how you can depend I'll be there every day. Not walk out. Show up with the money. You're right. I'm the one makes this marriage boring. But you're the one who needs for it to be boring. Because you, if you were left to your tricks, you would destroy the world. That's who you are.

NATALIE: The world? Would that include, like, Australia?

HENRY: You know what I'm talking about.

NATALIE: What do you want from me?

HENRY: Nothing.

NATALIE: I'm sorry.

HENRY: I can't want anything from you. And why not? You got no money left from your pay?

NATALIE: I'm still catching up the credit cards.

HENRY: Good luck. Now why do you want a joint checking account?

NATALIE: I just thought it would show respect.

HENRY: Don't waste my fucking time! Why do you want a joint checking account?

(She starts crying.)

What's this?

NATALIE: I'm scared.

HENRY: That I believe. Why?

NATALIE: I don't wanna say.

HENRY: Why not?

NATALIE: You'll judge me.

HENRY: Fuck that. I hate judges. That's not what I do. I'm an adversarial man. I've got a point of view and I take sides! Now why are you scared?

NATALIE: I saw something that couldn't be.

HENRY: Good for you.

NATALIE: You don't understand.

HENRY: Fine. You'll explain it to me.

NATALIE: I saw a ghost! Okay? I saw a ghost.

HENRY: What ghost? Whose ghost?

NATALIE: Tommy.

(Pause.)

HENRY: Where?

NATALIE: A coffee place. Middle of the day. I was with a friend. She saw him, too.

HENRY: A ghost.

NATALIE: Yes.

HENRY: Well, how 'bout that.

NATALIE: I know.

HENRY: That is some first-class stamp. That is a level of validation I didn't think I would ever get.

NATALIE: I guess it is.

HENRY: Say something to me.

NATALIE: I'm sorry.

HENRY: For what?

NATALIE: For not believing you when you told me you saw a ghost.

HENRY: You laughed in my face.

NATALIE: Well, of course I did. It seemed so . . .

HENRY: Crazy. I know. We're married married married. When's the trust kick in? When I see a ghost or when you see one?

NATALIE: All right. You've got a point.

HENRY: My mother came back.

NATALIE: All right, I believe you.

HENRY: It was the biggest moment in my life. It's the reason I'm not a junkie today. And you laughed in my face.

NATALIE: Well I'm sorry.

HENRY: She came right through the wall, busted my stereo all to shit! She had a number eight frying pan in her right hand. She said, "You stick that needle in your arm again, sonny boy, and I'll take your head off the payroll!" Looked me in the eye. It was love. It was love made her come back and save me. What made Tommy come back? Was it love?

NATALIE: Money.

HENRY *(Starts laughing)*: Money? What's Tommy gonna do with money? He's dead!

NATALIE: I owe him twenty-seven hundred dollars.

HENRY: That's a very specific amount.

NATALIE: I borrowed it from him.

HENRY: When? What for?

NATALIE: I bought my wedding dress with it.

(This stops Henry.)

HENRY: I thought your father bought you that?

(Natalie shakes her head.)

You went to Tommy? Why would you go to Tommy? Why didn't you come to me?

NATALIE: Oh Henry, you were in the middle of struggling yourself.

HENRY: You were through with Tommy! You broke his heart! Why would you ask him for money?

NATALIE: He had it.

HENRY: He didn't have it any more than I did. He was a janitor. He didn't even have clean clothes. Why him and not me?

NATALIE: I can't piece it together now. It made sense at the time.

HENRY: I knew there was something.

NATALIE: I didn't even know I was gonna do it, I just did it.

HENRY: There's always been something. A missing piece.

NATALIE: This has nothing to do with us.

HENRY: This has everything to do with us!

NATALIE: No, this was before. This was Tommy. I just wanted revenge.

HENRY: Revenge for what? You left him!

NATALIE: I thought I was going to talk to him, but then I got mad at him and I asked him for money to look good for you. Twenty-seven hundred dollars. It was all the money he had. And he gave it to me. I thought he wouldn't. That's why I asked for it. I thought that would be the break. But then he gave it to me.

HENRY: Did you fuck him?

NATALIE: Yes. It was before we were married.

(Henry grabs some clothes.)

HENRY: I'm not sleeping here tonight.

NATALIE: Don't leave me alone.

HENRY: Why not?

NATALIE: I'm scared.

HENRY: You know why you're scared?

NATALIE: He didn't love me.

HENRY: Did you love him?

NATALIE: No.

HENRY: That's fucked-up.

NATALIE: He treated me like an animal! He called me a whore! Every time! Like I was nothing!

HENRY: Then why'd you keep going back?

NATALIE: He had a hold on me.

HENRY: He still does.

NATALIE: He's dead!

HENRY: So what! You still want something from him.

NATALIE: He degraded me and I wanted back at him!

HENRY: To an endless point?

NATALIE: To the fucking grave.

HENRY: Looks like you didn't stop there. Looks like you dug him up.

NATALIE: Where you gonna sleep?

HENRY: Who said I'm gonna sleep?

NATALIE: Look! There's no need to go. This thing . . . It's the past!

HENRY: The past is real.

NATALIE: Where you going?

HENRY: Out to the world, my love.

NATALIE: What if he comes again? I don't want to be alone.

(Henry's dressed.)

HENRY: Hey, you're never alone. We just found that out. You sit here, you wait. Maybe I'll be back. Now here's a story come alive, right? What's gonna happen next? Let's turn the page.

(He exits. She cries. She stops. She reaches under the bed, grabs a small box, takes out a joint, and lights it. She takes a couple of hits. She goes over to the CD player, picks up a CD, and puts it on the boom box. Turns off the light. Street light floods the room. Music plays: Maybe Marcia Ball singing "Another Man's Woman." She takes another hit on the joint. The ghost, Tommy, appears backlit in the doorway. She sees him. She is not sur-

prised. Slowly, she gets up, goes to him. He meets her halfway. They begin to dance. Dreamy. Dreamy. Then he begins to strangle her. She tries to scream, can't. He roars at her.)

TOMMY: Where's my money, Natalie?! Where is it?! Where?!

(Blackout. Music out. She screams.
Lights up. Daytime. Natalie's in bed, awakening from a nightmare. She starts sobbing.)

NATALIE: Oh Tommy! Tommy!

(Music: Something like Irma Thomas singing "Time Is on My Side" begins to play. The lights fade ever so slowly.)

Scene 3

A scuffed, green metal desk, dirty venetian blinds, a couple of chairs. A middle-aged guy in a cheap suit, Sidney, sits behind the desk reading a book, chewing gum. A knock.

SIDNEY: Come in.

(Henry comes in. His clothes are wrinkled. He hasn't bathed.)

Henry.
HENRY: Ay, Sidney. Busy?
SIDNEY: As it's you, no. *(Hears something)* Did you hear that?
HENRY: What?
SIDNEY: Nothing. The goddamn hot water in this building, it's a presence. Come on, sit down.
HENRY: Thanks. Always with the book. What are you readin' now?
SIDNEY: *Casanova.*
HENRY: The lover.
SIDNEY: That's right. How are you doing with the *Crime and Punishment*?
HENRY: I'm marching through it. Sometimes it's good.

SIDNEY: It falls apart at the end. He goes to jail, his brain collapses, and he finds God. You're a little disheveled.

HENRY: A bit. *(Indicating the book)* So you're interested in love?

SIDNEY: Oh yeah.

HENRY: What do you think of a guy like that? So many women?

SIDNEY: Good for him. He was a true believer. And when he finally became cynical, which took him a long time to do, he didn't become cynical about the women. He became cynical about himself. *(Hears something again)* What *is* that sound?

HENRY: I don't hear anything.

SIDNEY: You're lucky. It's a curse to be sensitive.

HENRY: How do you know if you've become cynical about yourself?

SIDNEY: I think it starts when you begin to notice your own innocence.

HENRY: Have you had that experience?

SIDNEY: Never.

HENRY: You're not so tough.

SIDNEY: Please yourself. I love being underestimated.

HENRY: Are you superstitious?

SIDNEY: I won't walk under a ladder, but that's about the extent.

HENRY: I may not be able to tell you this story then.

SIDNEY: You're not baiting me, are you?

HENRY: No, no. I'm a little tired.

SIDNEY: Marital trouble?

HENRY: How'd you know?

SIDNEY: I'm a divorce lawyer. *(The phone rings. Sidney picks it up)* Yeah? Hold my calls. I'm with a potential client. *(Hangs up the phone)* Talk to me.

HENRY: Wait a minute.

SIDNEY: What she do?

HENRY: I'm not getting divorced.

SIDNEY: You're right. Let's stay away from the result. Let's look at the cause of your anguish.

HENRY: I guess that's the important thing. The core issue. Unfaithful, Sidney. She was unfaithful to me.

SIDNEY: Can you prove it?

HENRY: I don't need to.

SIDNEY: In this state you do.

HENRY: Look. This is not a consultation. I'm just talking to you.

SIDNEY: Forgive me. Old habits die hard. Had you set a precedent?

HENRY: For what?

SIDNEY: Were you unfaithful to her?

HENRY: No. Never.

SIDNEY: Well, there's your problem.

HENRY: What?

SIDNEY: Somebody had to do it. It's usually the man, but . . . It's physics. It's library science. The jobs will be filled, the roles will be played. *(Hears something)* There it is again, but you don't hear it, right? Forget it. Take my wife—I'm not gonna make the joke—Marcia Marie is totally, one thousand percent faithful to me.

HENRY: So do I extrapolate from that that you fuck around?

SIDNEY: In my first marriage, never! Never! I was a paragon. And my first wife flew on planes to fuck men. She would go vast distances and miss meals to bang a busboy in Council Bluffs. It was my fault. That was my job. And I didn't do it. I indulged in moral luxury. I was a wifely husband. And that ain't the job.

HENRY: What job?

SIDNEY: Manhood.

HENRY: I don't think of manhood as a job.

SIDNEY: It's a job. Done right, it's a tiring job. And women have a lot to do with what that job entails. Sure, women create. The womb. We all acknowledge the womb. But there's another side. And it's not pretty. There's a Hindu deity in India named Kali. The god of destruction. It's a woman. She's got a bloody sword and an appetite for decapitation. In the West, we call her "The Devouring Mother." Creation, destruction. Every woman has these two sides to her, and every man must deal with these two sides. Creation, destruction. You gotta orient a woman in such a way so as to be facing her creative parts. You want the creative parts. The destructive parts—you want those to be facing away. Towards a wall or an enemy or some-thing. Women consume, and they must be directed what to consume, or they may identify you as lunch. You've gotta point them. Like you would a bazooka. Like you would a chainsaw. You don't hold a chainsaw by the chain. Let me pull it together another way. Monogamy is like a forty-watt bulb. It works,

but it's not enough. Women used to come with goats and textiles. When they got upset, they worked on their textiles and
they yelled at their goats. Now they look around, no goats, no
textiles. All there is is some schmuck trying to read his news-
paper. All right, all right, here it is boiled down to nothing.
Don't bet the farm, Henry. That's what I'm trying to say. 'Cause
if a woman smells that you're betting the farm on her, you're
gonna lose the farm.

HENRY: Maybe you've been at this job too long.

SIDNEY: I didn't learn this on the job. This is home truth.

HENRY: I can't get divorced again.

SIDNEY: You don't have to get divorced. You know my wife Marcia
Marie, right?

HENRY: Yeah.

SIDNEY: What do you think of her?

HENRY: She's lovely. She's very nice.

SIDNEY: She's a bag of shit and I have to hold my nose to fuck her.

HENRY: Sidney, we're talking about your wife!

SIDNEY: And the mother of my children.

HENRY: You don't have children.

SIDNEY: Figure of speech.

HENRY: Look, I know you're . . . I admire you, Sidney, how you've
succeeded at work, the books. But I guess everybody falls
down . . .

SIDNEY: Fortunately, I don't look to Marcia Marie to pit my peach.

HENRY: How did this become about your marriage?

SIDNEY: I've got another woman for that and she's better than a
quart of blood.

HENRY: So you do cheat.

SIDNEY: It's how I passed the bar.

HENRY: There's no way to cheat on the bar.

SIDNEY: I'll choose not to correct you.

HENRY: Even if there is, I wouldn't want it. It wouldn't be right.

SIDNEY: Right? You poor bastard, they've got you by the balls. Right
and wrong, that's the corral they use to keep the cows out of
the house. A man like you should know better. A man who came
from the depths. Henry, we're lawyers. We do not traffic in right
and wrong. Come on. That's for chumps. That's for clients.

HENRY: I think Justice exists.

SIDNEY: Good for you. Meet me on Mount Sinai . . . we'll do a dance. Answer me this, Moses. What is morality?

HENRY: It's . . . I know it when I see it.

SIDNEY: Very good. So do I. It's a franchise. Morality is a chain restaurant. You go there because you know what you're gonna get. One burger. You don't have to think. You don't have to invent a response to the unknown. It's a lot like being dead except you're eating. I had a vision about six months ago. It changed my life. I'd just lost a case. A woman with three kids. One autistic. Her husband stole everything and I couldn't stop him because she was moral and he wasn't. It got me down. I went walking on Jay Street. I looked at the malformed people who actually inhabit this world. And there among them I saw a broken old lady, derelict, starving, blind, ignored, an outcast sitting on the sidewalk. And then, awful, I realized I knew her. Henry, her name was Justice. Everybody just walked around her, pretended she didn't exist. But I saw her. And I resolved, right there, on that street, looking at that lost woman, that I was not going to be her. I was going to get what I need to survive. Irrespective of anybody else's idea of good or right. Two days later, I was down at Borough Hall for a preconference. This clerk was busting my chops and I went out for a breather to the men's room. When outta the ladies room came this girl. And though I didn't know her, I recognized her. Like she was wearing an identifying shackle. She had a limp. It was the sexiest thing I've ever seen.

HENRY: Look, Sidney, I was going to ask you for advice, but you're further out on the peninsula than me.

SIDNEY: You think you can get everything you need from one woman?

HENRY: I don't know. What is everything?

SIDNEY: Good question! What's inside you? What's the scope of Henry? What do you include? Think about it.

HENRY: I am thinking, but what are you doing, man? It sounds to me like you got burned by your first wife, so then you just chose to be a clown or something.

SIDNEY: I am not a clown.

HENRY: I just mean it seems like you're making fun of your own heart. Out of this pain. Like smiling despair or words like that.

SIDNEY: I'm not in despair. I'm not going to kill myself. So what, life is not this pretty thing. I still want it. I want to live. You've seen what passes through this office. You know what's left of love when life is done with it. Bones. We don't have to fear the whirlwind, Henry, we *are* the whirlwind. Now you can go with that, or you can succumb. I've made my choice. I lie. I steal. I cheat. I've chosen life. And I am having a very good time. Marcia Marie and me: It was us. We were living in a TV show. A pilot that wasn't gonna get picked up. I was playing a part. I still play it, but now I know it's just a mask, not the real me at all.

HENRY: But then what are you doing? Why are you still married?

SIDNEY: I'll tell you why! Revenge!

HENRY: For what?

SIDNEY: All that time I towed the line! Retribution requires a recipient. I need Marcia Marie to lie to, steal from, cheat on! At this point, that's what Marcia Marie is for. She makes it wrong. And wrong is right.

HENRY: Wrong is right.

SIDNEY: Don't repeat me to me. Maybe once in your life you're supposed to do something hard. Some fork in the road. Your soul-saving contribution. But the rest of the time—to call a duck a duck—life is a very dirty party.

HENRY: You're talking too much to be right.

SIDNEY: I'm talking about the thing in all people that you may call evil that has just as much right to expression as anything else in you! I'm talking about not being on your deathbed choking on emotional pus because you didn't once speak. Am I talking about evil? Who cares?! Why did I give you *Crime and Punishment*, Henry? What is conscience? I think it's loneliness. *(He is surprised by tears. Gets them under control)* Society banishes the man who lives by his own right and wrong. Maybe I do want to be understood. Maybe because you've stumbled onto some kind of hypocrisy in your marriage, you may be open to understanding me. And this thing of mine with this girl. This girl, all the black scum of my long beleaguered heart, she eats. I can't tell you what I've said to her, done to her. The literally most horrible things I could think of! And she comes back for more. She's grateful. God bless her. Yes, I mention God! Because it is like a miracle. We found each other. She's sweet, she's like a kid. She was sad about this pin she lost. I bought her another one. When I give it to her, it will make her day.

(Sidney takes out an alligator pin and shows it to Henry.)

HENRY: Is that an alligator?

SIDNEY *(Throws it on his desk)*: Some fuckin' reptile. Do you know why I went into matrimonial law?

HENRY: The money?

SIDNEY: Don't be an idiot! It's never about money! YOU MEAN YOU REALLY DON'T HEAR THAT SOUND?! I went into matrimonial law to do for others what I didn't have the courage to do for myself. Sever the conventional bond. I was the most cynical bastard in the world. 'Cause I knew there was no love to be had. All the bitter disappointment of my marriage bed, I turned on the spouses of my clients. That bitch! That bastard! And then I would go home and kiss that fat pink ass of empty virtue, my wife.

HENRY: But your wife is skinny.

SIDNEY: But I think of her as fat. Despicable! I was a despicable man! I did much harm. But no more. Because now when a man or woman comes in my office and sits here and tells me their dreams have come to nothing, I have something to give them. I have hope.

HENRY: I don't want revenge. I just want my wife.

SIDNEY: Wake up. You got your wife. That's the problem. She's there. *(The phone rings)* Excuse me. *(Answers the phone)* What do I pay you for? To not listen? Oh. All right. *(Pause. Turns away and speaks in a voice too low to be heard)* Yes? Yes, that's right. Why do you want to know? I see. This happened recently? That's terrible. Well no, I don't think I do. Really? But I'm sure I'm not the only one. Of course. Of course. Yeah. Would you mind, I'm in the middle of business. Yeah.

(He hangs up the phone, sits quietly a long moment, peaceful. Then he tears the phone off his desk and throws it violently against the wall.)

God! Jesus! What the fuck!

HENRY: What the hell are you doing?!

SIDNEY: That girl. The girl with the limp. She shot herself. She named me in a note, and then she shot herself.

(Sidney breaks down. Henry comforts him.)

Oh my God, did I do this? Am I responsible?

HENRY: Shh. Shh. Take it easy. Take it easy now.

SIDNEY: And I denied I knew her.

HENRY: That's reflex.

SIDNEY: I gave her the gun!

HENRY: You did?

SIDNEY: It was supposed to protect her.

(We hear a pronounced thump.)

Do you hear it now? Do you hear that thing now?

HENRY: Yeah. What is that?

(Another thump. Horrified, Sidney realizes what it is.)

SIDNEY: It's her limp! It's Celeste! It's her limp! Jesus, she's coming for me!

(Suddenly, Celeste rises out of her bed in the corner. She is dressed in white. There's a bloodstain. She points at Sidney, who goes white with fear, plastering himself against the opposite wall.)

CELESTE: Sidney.

SIDNEY: I'm sorry, Celeste! I'm sorry! I'm sorry!

CELESTE: Listen to me.

SIDNEY: That I degraded you to this point of destruction!

CELESTE: I've come to tell you . . .

SIDNEY: What can I do to make it right?!

CELESTE *(Raising both her hands in supplication)*: It was not your fault. You were the good part of my life.

SIDNEY: But then why did you do it? Why?

(Celeste wheels on Henry, points an accusing finger, and says:)

CELESTE: ASK YOUR WIFE!

(Blackout. Music: Something like Charley Musselwhite singing "Baby Will You Please Help Me" kicks in.)

Scene 4

A kitchen table, sun coming in. Sidney is sitting at the table. Marcia Marie, who wears sexless, neat clothes, is making coffee in a Mr. Coffee machine. She hasn't been happy for a long time. A silence hangs over them.

MARCIA MARIE: I have a confession. I'm disappointed you're home. I like this time for myself.

SIDNEY: Aaa. There was an incident at work.

MARCIA MARIE: What?

SIDNEY: I don't know.

MARCIA MARIE: Did you get fired?

SIDNEY: No. Nobody's gonna fire me, Marcia Marie. I'm a very successful man.

MARCIA MARIE: Did I say different?

SIDNEY: Something.

MARCIA MARIE: I saw a pair of pants today that were very you. I'll tell you where they are. You should go and look at them.

SIDNEY: I can dress myself.

MARCIA MARIE: Did I say different?

SIDNEY: There was a phone call. There was a phone call at work.

MARCIA MARIE: I didn't call you.

SIDNEY: I didn't say you did.

MARCIA MARIE: You can't accuse me of hounding you.

SIDNEY: I'm not.

MARCIA MARIE: I never call except when I have no choice. It's not like the old days when I used to make what you called pointless calls. Distracting you from the great work.

SIDNEY: Look. This is a tough day for me. Could you lay off?

MARCIA MARIE: Well, this is a tough day for me, too. Maybe you want to go out for a walk till it's the time you usually come home?

SIDNEY: No. If you want somebody to go out, why don't you go out?

MARCIA MARIE: Me? I'm not going anywhere. I'm wiped.

SIDNEY: Wiped from what?

MARCIA MARIE: It's tiring for me when you're here.

SIDNEY: I'm here every morning and every night.

MARCIA MARIE: Not every night.

SIDNEY: Most nights.

MARCIA MARIE: So you can imagine how tired I am.

SIDNEY: Well, this is my home. This is where I can go.

MARCIA MARIE: You have the office.

SIDNEY: Yes, I have an office and then I come home. Those are the two poles of my universe.

MARCIA MARIE: Well, I only have one pole, this is it, and I deserve time alone. You make me nervous.

SIDNEY: You mean just by being alive?

MARCIA MARIE: During the day. In my kitchen. Yes. So I'm making coffee. Do you want some or not?

SIDNEY: Won't coffee make you more nervous?

MARCIA MARIE: At this point, I don't think so. I'm too wiped.

SIDNEY: But from what?!

MARCIA MARIE: You. Your aura. There's only so much of your aura I can take.

SIDNEY: Well, back at ya.

MARCIA MARIE: But I didn't come to your office. You came to my kitchen.

SIDNEY: And did what?

MARCIA MARIE: Don't I deserve anything?

SIDNEY: You know, I hate to smack your piñata, but this is my kitchen, too. I paid for this kitchen.

MARCIA MARIE: I paid for this kitchen.

SIDNEY: With what?

MARCIA MARIE: My ass.

SIDNEY: It's our apartment.

MARCIA MARIE: I deserve a room.

SIDNEY: You have your own bathroom.

MARCIA MARIE: Are you trying to drive me into the bathroom now?

SIDNEY: I'm not trying to drive you anywhere. You're trying to drive me out of my own apartment.

MARCIA MARIE: During the day.

SIDNEY: Day, night, what's the difference?

MARCIA MARIE: You don't know the difference between day and night?

SIDNEY: A.M., P.M., shelter is shelter.

MARCIA MARIE *(To an audience member)*: I'm sorry.

SIDNEY *(To another audience member)*: Pardon me.

MARCIA MARIE: Pressure.

SIDNEY: Gas bag.

MARCIA MARIE: I've made peace with the idea of part of you part of the time.

SIDNEY: I've made concessions, too.

MARCIA MARIE: Are you looking for further concessions from me?

SIDNEY: I've come to recognize the need for some form of end of you and beginning of other things, okay?

MARCIA MARIE: Why won't you give me what I want?

SIDNEY: And what is that?

MARCIA MARIE: Space.

SIDNEY: Are there definite limits to the amount of space you need?

MARCIA MARIE: I have none.

SIDNEY: What are we talking about?! What about the . . .

MARCIA MARIE: I have nothing. I'm irrelevant. And you remind me. And I can't be reminded all the time. I need breaks.

SIDNEY: To do what?

MARCIA MARIE: Daydream.

SIDNEY: About what?

MARCIA MARIE: Big picture? Goods and services.

SIDNEY: You know, you could long and ache and pine for other things besides goods and services.

117

MARCIA MARIE: Oh but no. You have limited me to dreaming about goods and services, God help me.

SIDNEY: You don't need God. You need a concierge.

MARCIA MARIE: I need my soul.

SIDNEY: Don't look at me.

MARCIA MARIE: I am looking at you. I'm like a check you never endorsed.

SIDNEY: Why should it be up to me to cash you?

MARCIA MARIE: An undeposited check, at a certain point, the bank doesn't honor it anymore. And when the bank doesn't honor you, honey, and you're a check, well, that's bleak.

SIDNEY: Look. You might as well know. I've had a big shock. Never mind about what. But I'm not doing too terrific. I'm having some suicidal ideas.

MARCIA MARIE: I have suicidal ideas.

SIDNEY: Are you gonna vie with me now for the right to be suicidal?

MARCIA MARIE: I'm going to defend myself.

SIDNEY: Against what?

MARCIA MARIE: Your feelings. Your emotional supremacy.

SIDNEY: That's just me talking. I don't wanna rule over you. I want it not to matter what I do.

MARCIA MARIE: Well, it does matter.

(A relenting. He turns away, thinks about it, and finally gives her the small gift box with the alligator pin.)

SIDNEY: Look. Here.

MARCIA MARIE: What's this?

SIDNEY: A present.

MARCIA MARIE: A pin.

SIDNEY: It's nothing. It's an alligator.

MARCIA MARIE: White enamel. It goes with everything I have.

SIDNEY: Don't make a big thing, put it away.

MARCIA MARIE: It's exquisite.

SIDNEY: It's just costume jewelry. A little doodad.

MARCIA MARIE: You thought of me.

SIDNEY: I don't know what I was thinking about.

MARCIA MARIE: You were out . . .

SIDNEY (*Overlapping*): Put it away!

MARCIA MARIE: You thought of me.

SIDNEY (*Overlapping*): Put it away!

MARCIA MARIE: You went into a store—

SIDNEY: Forget it.

MARCIA MARIE: Thank you.

SIDNEY: It's nothing. Forget it.

(*Touched by her perception of a tender gesture, Marcia Marie throws herself at Sidney. He tries to get away.*)

MARCIA MARIE: Let's go on a trip. Let's go on a trip.

SIDNEY (*Overlapping*): Get your hands off me.

MARCIA MARIE: Please! Please! Please!

SIDNEY: Get your hands off me! Don't make a big thing I said.

(*Suddenly, a sexual moment. He grabs her lustfully. Violent grinding. She moans. But he panics, tears free.*)

This is why I wanna kill myself. You're a trap! I feel a move of my hand could topple your world.

MARCIA MARIE: That's right. And that's a responsibility.

SIDNEY: Well, I reject that responsibility! In order for me to save you, I have to kill me! And I wanna live! I wanna live. All right. I'm gonna take the steps necessary to stop having these dark ideas. I want a divorce.

MARCIA MARIE: And that's not going to happen. Do you want coffee?

SIDNEY: Can I ask you? What is this? I mean, over time? What are we doing?

MARCIA MARIE: Big picture? We've been killing each other.

SIDNEY: But why? Why would we do that?

MARCIA MARIE: No guts, I guess.

SIDNEY: For what?

MARCIA MARIE: Freedom.

SIDNEY: What would you know about freedom?

MARCIA MARIE (*Feigns a limp to make her point*): Oh boy, a slave in her shackles knows about freedom!

SIDNEY: Don't do that. Don't do that.

MARCIA MARIE: Why not?

SIDNEY: Are you superstitious?

MARCIA MARIE: Very.

SIDNEY: I didn't know that.

MARCIA MARIE: How else can I explain my life except by thinking that I suffer under a curse of your causing.

SIDNEY: But why me?! What did I do?

MARCIA MARIE: You destroy marriages for a living.

SIDNEY: Whereas you do it gratuitously. You're the inspiration for my work, Marcia Marie. I see myself as saving people. I see myself as goddamn Robin Hood!

MARCIA MARIE: Robin Hood was a glorified thug. As are you.

SIDNEY: I perform a service.

MARCIA MARIE: So do I.

SIDNEY: What?

MARCIA MARIE: I keep you off the market.

SIDNEY: So you're containing me.

MARCIA MARIE: Yes.

SIDNEY: And I'm containing you.

MARCIA MARIE: Containing and invading. You're in my kitchen now. In the daytime.

SIDNEY: Each of us in a smaller and smaller bottle.

MARCIA MARIE: No, you're free.

SIDNEY: But that's not what you said before. That's a contradiction.

MARCIA MARIE: What, are you trying to catch me up?

SIDNEY: I'm trying to understand.

MARCIA MARIE: No.

SIDNEY: You won't let me understand.

MARCIA MARIE: You understand. But I'm not going to help you.

SIDNEY: Why not?

(She goes for the coffee in the pantry.)

MARCIA MARIE: I have more reasons than there are fish in the sea.

SIDNEY: Name one.

MARCIA MARIE: You know.

SIDNEY: No, I do not know.

MARCIA MARIE: You have been having an affair.

SIDNEY: No, I haven't.

MARCIA MARIE *(Pours hot coffee on his hand)*: And you're a liar.

(He yips and jumps away.)

SIDNEY: I don't wanna do this.

MARCIA MARIE: What?

SIDNEY: Actually talk to you.

MARCIA MARIE: No, you don't.

SIDNEY: Or if I do want to talk, this is not the topic. Or even if this is the topic, I can't let you poison the last well I have to drink from. I'm gonna save myself.

MARCIA MARIE: And you think I'm fat.

SIDNEY: What are you talking about?! You're skinny!

MARCIA MARIE: What are YOU talking about? I'm fat! I'm shaking with fat!

SIDNEY: You're a rail, you're a stick, you're practically gaunt!

MARCIA MARIE: But you think of me as fat, don't you!

SIDNEY: Who said that? No!

MARCIA MARIE: Then why don't you fuck me?

SIDNEY: What are you talking about? I do fuck you.

MARCIA MARIE: No, you don't.

SIDNEY: This is surreal.

MARCIA MARIE: You've changed the order of things. That's what men do. They rearrange the truth.

SIDNEY: Whereas you don't even bother with it.

MARCIA MARIE: I am all about the truth.

SIDNEY: No. You are all about cruelty. Every piece of toast in your breadbasket is buttered with cruelty.

MARCIA MARIE: You want some toast? I could make some.

SIDNEY: Are you serious?

MARCIA MARIE: Yeah.

SIDNEY: Jesus. Domesticity.

MARCIA MARIE: You want some toast or not?

SIDNEY: No, I don't want any fucking toast! And you wear those goddamn ugly clothes!

MARCIA MARIE: What's the matter with my clothes?

SIDNEY: They say you're married.

MARCIA MARIE: I am married.

SIDNEY: Those clothes say you fuck by the numbers.

MARCIA MARIE: But I don't fuck by the numbers 'cause you don't fuck me.

SIDNEY: What are you talkin' about? We fuck two-point-eight times a week.

MARCIA MARIE: And you say I'm by the numbers. I don't have sex with you, Sidney. You leave your body, I abandon mine, what's left fucks.

SIDNEY: Well, I hope those faceless homunculi have fun. Whoever they are.

MARCIA MARIE: I have sex with a zombie.

SIDNEY: That's nothing. I have sex with death!

MARCIA MARIE: So you're dead. Lie down.

SIDNEY: I didn't say I was dead, I said I have sex with death.

MARCIA MARIE: Who is she?

SIDNEY: You.

MARCIA MARIE: Easy. Glib. Prick. Just remember. It's not my fault how you feel about who you turned out to be. A flop.

SIDNEY: My life hasn't reached the point of verdict.

MARCIA MARIE: Your life isn't on trial, Sidney. There's nothing to argue about. There's nothing to rule on. You have no case. You're a flop.

SIDNEY: You don't get to say.

MARCIA MARIE: Who knows you better than me?

SIDNEY: You don't know me.

MARCIA MARIE: All I know is you.

SIDNEY: No. The problem is you think I'm you and you detest yourself.

MARCIA MARIE: No, I know who I detest and I know why I detest him. I just can't believe I married him, that's all! I just can't believe I'm here!

SIDNEY: I can't believe I'm here, either! It's implausible that I'm here!

MARCIA MARIE: It's funny!

SIDNEY: Ha. Ha. But why are you here if you don't wanna be here?!

MARCIA MARIE: To make sure you don't get away with it.

SIDNEY: With what?

MARCIA MARIE: No more. Nothing more to say.

SIDNEY: There are people . . . There is a woman . . . There *was* a woman, who loved me.

MARCIA MARIE: So. Finally. There it is. You admit it.

SIDNEY: Yes. All right. I admit it. I admit the dirty secret that somebody loved me, yes.

MARCIA MARIE: Who?

SIDNEY: Never mind, it's not important. She's gone. She's out of the picture. But without her, the good news is, you become impossible to bear.

MARCIA MARIE: Who was she?

SIDNEY: What do you care?

MARCIA MARIE: Who was she?

SIDNEY: I'm not tellin' you her name.

MARCIA MARIE: Who was she?

SIDNEY: She's gone.

MARCIA MARIE: She ditched you. Well, of course. Sooner or later, they all wake up.

SIDNEY: Not exactly. She's dead.

MARCIA MARIE: She killed herself.

SIDNEY: How'd you know that?

MARCIA MARIE: That's why you were thinking about suicide. Figures. You're so suggestible.

SIDNEY: No, it doesn't figure! It's a tragedy!

MARCIA MARIE: Tragedy is when you fall from a height. Not when a homewrecker hangs herself!

SIDNEY: She didn't hang herself!

MARCIA MARIE: But she was a homewrecker. How did she do it? What did she do? Pills? Jump off a building? No. Takes guts to jump. Or did she shoot herself?

SIDNEY: Are you a fucking witch?

MARCIA MARIE: No. You're the spiritual one. You and your books. You left me nothing but the flesh.

SIDNEY: I'm not talking about this with you anymore.

MARCIA MARIE: So she shot herself. Did she leave a note? Did she name you in the note? Sidney?

SIDNEY: I'm not talking.

MARCIA MARIE: Are you in trouble?

SIDNEY: Potentially. I gave her . . . I had given her a gun.

MARCIA MARIE: You stupid ass. Where did you get a gun?

SIDNEY: Some creep. A domestic violence dispute. I don't think it's traceable to me.

MARCIA MARIE: You didn't kill her, did you?

SIDNEY: No.

MARCIA MARIE: Did you?

SIDNEY: No!

MARCIA MARIE: You may need me. The credibility I bring. Or just my brain. I'll do that for you. But what was her name?

SIDNEY: I feel like if I tell you her name . . . Maybe this is that fork in the road for me. The one time I'm supposed to do something hard. Or I'll be damned.

MARCIA MARIE: I'm damned. Why shouldn't you be? You stole my soul.

SIDNEY: Go ahead. Frisk me! I don't have it. I don't have your soul. You've ransacked me looking for it. You wrecked me.

MARCIA MARIE: I was lonely.

SIDNEY: You were lonely when I met you.

MARCIA MARIE: Marriage is supposed to end that.

SIDNEY: You were misinformed about the nature of the institution.

MARCIA MARIE: You never gave me a chance. Who was she?

SIDNEY: I should respect this thing she did.

MARCIA MARIE: Blowing her brains out?

SIDNEY: No, something else. Maybe this is that fork in the road for me. I shouldn't betray her name. Maybe you're right. Maybe this marriage is my doing. If it is, I'm sorry. Maybe I just didn't have enough love to conquer all.

MARCIA MARIE: You never gave me a chance. You shut me out.

SIDNEY: No.

MARCIA MARIE: You shut me out. Because your first wife was untrue. You showed up in my life a light-hearted-looking man. But your smile and your easiness came out of despair. I didn't understand that.

SIDNEY: But I could've melted. You could've melted me. Like the sun melts the snow.

MARCIA MARIE: I'm just a woman, Sidney. I'm not Spring.

SIDNEY: I've been afraid of you for so long.

MARCIA MARIE: Why would you be scared of me?

SIDNEY: I don't know.

MARCIA MARIE *(Suddenly explodes)*: Who was she?! Tell me her fucking name!

SIDNEY: No, I won't! It's mine! She loved me! I can't let you touch it!

MARCIA MARIE: You know I'll find out! If I can't have a room, neither can you! I'll just hammer away at you until you give it up! I'll get at it and I'll piss on it!

SIDNEY: I'm leaving you!

MARCIA MARIE: You're not going anywhere! You gave me a pin.

SIDNEY: Forget the pin. Some good's gotta come of this!

MARCIA MARIE: Of what?!

SIDNEY: Her sacrifice.

MARCIA MARIE: You talk about her sacrifice to me? I sold my ass for a kitchen!

SIDNEY: But why did you do that?

MARCIA MARIE: I didn't think I could do better.

SIDNEY: And you don't even have clear title to the kitchen.

MARCIA MARIE: In the eyes of God, this is my kitchen. In the eyes of God, you are my husband.

SIDNEY: You are a materialist. Materialists go mad. They break their possessions to prove that they own them. I'm going to leave you, I'm going to temple, and then I'm going to the police. I won't let you kill anymore. She used to say she could smell murder on me. I knew what she was smelling was you.

(Marcia Marie grabs a butcher knife from a drawer.)

MARCIA MARIE: You're staying here. With me. Till death. That's the vow! And you're gonna keep it!

SIDNEY: Put down that knife!

MARCIA MARIE: You think you can humiliate me?

SIDNEY: Get a hold of yourself!

MARCIA MARIE: I'll do it! I'll do it! I'll do it!

(She lunges for him three times. He gets hold of her knife arm. She kicks at his legs while she struggles. Sidney cries, terrified.)

SIDNEY: Stop! Stop! What are you doing?

MARCIA MARIE: You're not going to her!

SIDNEY: She's dead!

MARCIA MARIE: You think I wanted to have this be my life? I. Want. Happiness!

(He gets the knife. She tries to smack him, but she's too weak now. He's panting.)

SIDNEY: The pursuit of happiness doesn't look like this.

(He throws the knife on the table.)

I'm leaving you.

(He goes to the door, opens it. She picks up the knife. She poises it to stab herself in the breast.)

MARCIA MARIE: If you walk out that door, I'm shoving this right through my heart. And you can explain two dead women in one day.

(Sidney hesitates, and then gives the name up.)

SIDNEY: Celeste. Her name was Celeste. I bought the pin for her.

(Sidney exits, slamming the door behind him. Marcia Marie stands there with the knife.)

MARCIA MARIE *(Yelling at the closed door)*: I want all the money! All of it!

(She looks at herself in the knife blade and recoils with recognition.)

My mother!

(Blackout.)

Scene 5

Lights up. Natalie's sitting in Henry's chair, sleeping. Daytime. The door opens. It's Henry. He comes in with a paper deli bag. Natalie starts awake and blurts out:

NATALIE: Tommy?
HENRY: Tommy huh?
NATALIE: Henry.
HENRY: Disappointed?

(She rushes to him.)

NATALIE: Oh no! What a night I've had!
HENRY: I hear ya.
NATALIE: What's in the bag?
HENRY: Coffee.
NATALIE: I could have made you coffee.
HENRY: You could have closed the front door, but you left it open again.
NATALIE: He came back.
HENRY: Who?
NATALIE: Tommy. He tried to kill me. Look at my neck!
HENRY: I don't see anything.

(She rushes to a mirror, looks at her neck, finds nothing.)

NATALIE: You don't? I couldn't breathe!
HENRY: Can you breathe now?
NATALIE: Yeah.
HENRY: Just a panic attack.
NATALIE: He was here!
HENRY: I believe you. It's not that.
NATALIE: What have you been doing when you were out?
HENRY: I saw Sidney. We had a talk. You know, I don't want to be Sidney.

(He goes to the CD player.)

Secret music again.

NATALIE: You seem strange.

HENRY: Do I?

(He pulls out three envelopes and throws them on the bed.)

Let's get to it. I put together these three envelopes. You may wanna open this one.

NATALIE: What is it?

HENRY: Twenty-seven hundred dollars.

NATALIE: Thanks.

HENRY: Now you may wanna take that, and you may not. If you take it, you're in debt to me. That's one way to go.

NATALIE: I could pay off my credit cards with this.

HENRY: What about your dead boy Tommy? Gotta pay him back.

NATALIE: I know. I'm just saying.

HENRY: Or you don't have to take the money from me. You could take the second envelope.

NATALIE: What's that one?

HENRY: An application for a joint checking account.

NATALIE: Really?

HENRY: Yeah. Then it would be our money. You could make a with-drawal. You wouldn't be in debt to anybody. You could go that way.

NATALIE: What's in the third envelope?

HENRY: That? That's an action for a divorce.

NATALIE: A divorce?

HENRY: If you choose that envelope, then we divide up our assets, and what you do is no longer my business. So. Natalie. What's it gonna be? Which envelope?

(She looks in the mirror again.)

NATALIE: I can't believe there's no mark! It seemed so real! Maybe you're right. Maybe it was just anxiety.

HENRY: What's it gonna be? The divorce, the account, or the cash?

NATALIE: Well, there's a logistical problem, isn't there?

HENRY: How do you mean?

NATALIE: To give the money back.

HENRY: Burn it.

NATALIE: Burn twenty-seven hundred dollars?

HENRY: Yeah.

NATALIE: Would that work?

HENRY: Fuck if I know.

NATALIE: I think you should put it back in the bank.

HENRY: That's not one of these three envelopes. That's us, no joint checking, married, with you in debt to a dead guy. I walked out on that deal last night.

NATALIE: But he's dead. It's too late to pay him back.

HENRY: Tell him that.

NATALIE: Well, I don't want to be out twenty-seven hundred dollars.

HENRY: Okay. So you want a divorce.

NATALIE: I didn't say that!

HENRY: I'm not going to be married like this anymore. I'm not going to be married to a woman who's only half here.

NATALIE: I'm here.

HENRY: Yeah, but you keep forgettin' to close the door.

NATALIE: What's your point?

HENRY: What about Tommy?

NATALIE: He's dead. That's the truth of it.

HENRY: The truth, huh?

NATALIE: That's right.

HENRY: I know you, Natalie. I know what you do in the name of the truth.

NATALIE: What?

HENRY: Serve yourself.

NATALIE: The truth is what it is.

HENRY: What about Justice?

NATALIE: What about it?

HENRY: Which side you on?

NATALIE: My side.

HENRY: You know what I think? There's two kinds of people. The ones that seek, and the ones that hide.

NATALIE (*Overlapping*): I'm not hiding from anything.

129

HENRY: But Justice finds you, you know? That's what *Crime and Punishment*'s about. You do shit, the clock starts ticking.

NATALIE: Don't talk to me like you're an adult and I'm not. I tell the truth and I pay the price! There should be more people like me.

HENRY: There's plenty of people like you.

NATALIE: Bullshit! Most people lie!

HENRY: You take care of yourself at the expense of everybody else and call it honesty! If that's the truth, then I hate the truth. That truth has no heart. It's ignorant, it's vicious. It's not the human part of people. Now I presented you with three envelopes and I'm asking you to choose.

NATALIE: You're not asking me! You're a bully! You're the inhuman one! And you know what I say? I say fuck you and fuck your little envelopes. Your little envelopes give me a pain in my ass. You've done nothing always but control me and dominate me with that checking account number and now you're laying out my future like three doors on a game show, and that's inhuman to me! You push me around, Henry. And it's not respectful! I have devoted myself to you and revolved around you, and I will not be given choices that I have to choose from. You are a making a crisis when there's nothing wrong!

HENRY: These envelopes, which I cooked up in my fear and my loneliness as a way of dealing with you may be as clumsy and crude as me, but you will not ignore them. You got one foot in and one foot out. You can talk till you're blue. Things can't stay like they are.

NATALIE: You scared me to death with those divorce papers!

HENRY: I'm presenting you with choices I can live with.

NATALIE: If you can live with divorce, then *you've* got one foot out. Your first wife ripped you off and I've been payin' in blood ever since. You've never trusted me!

HENRY: And I was right. You were lying from the get-go.

NATALIE: 'Cause I knew you wouldn't understand.

HENRY: What's to understand? Your wedding dress?

NATALIE: That was before we were married.

HENRY: Well, we're married now.

NATALIE: Are we?

HENRY: I'm here.

NATALIE: Well, I'm here, too.

HENRY: No you're not.

NATALIE: Yes I am.

HENRY: What about Tommy?

NATALIE: What about him?

HENRY: You've been carrying a torch for this dead guy.

NATALIE: No!

HENRY: Keepin' his dead ass alive.

NATALIE: Bull!

HENRY: Secret music.

NATALIE: Big deal.

HENRY: Steppin' out on me with fuckin' Frankenstein.

NATALIE: You're nuts!

HENRY: Let him go.

NATALIE: He's dead.

HENRY: He's here.

NATALIE: He's dead.

HENRY: He's here.

NATALIE *(Hardens)*: I didn't see a ghost.

(Tommy's arm smashes through the door and grabs Natalie by the throat. She screams.)

Oh my God!

HENRY *(Simultaneously)*: Ho! There he is. There's the deadmeat motherfucker himself!

NATALIE: Help!

HENRY: Let her go!

NATALIE: Help!

HENRY: Let her go!

NATALIE: Help!

HENRY: I command you to let her go!

NATALIE: He's not listening to you!

HENRY: Obstinate fucking zombie voodoo motherfucker! Let! Her! Go!

(Henry pulls her free of the hand; takes her a few feet away.)

NATALIE: I'm fine, I'm fine, I'm fine. Let me go!

(Henry lets her go. She flies backward, as if against her will, until Tommy's hand is again around her neck.)

HELP!

HENRY: I can't save you. You don't want to be saved.

NATALIE: Yes I do!

HENRY: Say there's a ghost!

NATALIE: Okay, there's a ghost.

(Tommy releases her.)

What does he want from me?

HENRY: What do you think he wants? He wants the money.

NATALIE: No!

(The ghost force pulls her back into the strangle again. She screams.)

HENRY: The past isn't done with till you PAY!

NATALIE: I don't want to give him the money! It's mine! I want it to be mine!

HENRY: That's not the same thing.

NATALIE: I want it to be!

HENRY: Wake the fuck up and pay the man his money!

(She pulls herself free of the hand. The door opens. Tommy stands there. We can't see his face. She gets the envelope and hands it over. Tommy takes it.)

NATALIE: All right. Goddammit. I'll get you your goddamn fucking blood money. Here's your money you cheap bastard. Go back to hell. Now go away!

(She slams the door, and leans against it.)

(To Henry) I'm sorry I cheated on you with that guy.

HENRY: I know. You gotta grow up, Natalie.

NATALIE: I know.

HENRY: I can't be going through this once a week. I need help. Life's too hard. It's too lonely.

NATALIE: What do you want?

HENRY: How 'bout love?

NATALIE: Okay.

HENRY: What do you want?

NATALIE: I want a joint checking account.

HENRY: Okay.

NATALIE: That fucking Tommy. Why did I ever have to meet him? And why did he have to be poor?

HENRY: Sit down.

NATALIE: And why couldn't I just take his money and forget it?

HENRY: Because what went on between you and Tommy, that had nothing to do with money. It had to do with love.

NATALIE: I know. I know.

HENRY: It was me. Your marriage to me. That was about money.

NATALIE: Ah. Henry.

HENRY: Stability. You married me for stability.

NATALIE: If I did, is that wrong?

HENRY: Oh baby, it haunts you.

NATALIE: What is marriage?

HENRY: I don't know.

NATALIE: Me neither.

HENRY: Wanna find out?

NATALIE: Okay.

(The other door falls with a crash. Celeste's ghost is standing there.)

CELESTE: Natalie, you lying bitch! Where's my white enamel alligator pin?! Where is it?!

HENRY: Oh yeah, this is the other thing we have to talk about.

(Blackout.)

END OF PLAY

Sailor's Song

This play is dedicated to my sister Bunny.

Preface

We must remember so much about the history of thought in order to achieve a meaningful experience of life. Cynicism was a school of Greek philosophy. They believed that one should live a virtuous life, eschew wealth and status, in order to find happiness. The Stoics built upon this thought. They characterized the universe as guided and inhabited by an intelligent, organizing force. Again, they emphasized the importance of living virtuously. They added to this idea acceptance, acceptance of a greater intelligence at work than one's own. In my play, the uncle, the older man, has leapt over pain, has tried to cheat his way past grief, by inundating his senses with sensual pleasure, and his mind with emotionally glib locutions. He acknowledges the ultimate unavoidable power of Fate, but nevertheless, being only a man, attempts to run away. It is all in vain. There is no way around the deep agonies of life. No philosophy can protect you from a broken heart. No liquor can medicate away the tears of loss. The modern use of the word "cynic" really describes a person on the run from the central emotional experience of being sentient and mortal. The two men in this play are struggling with the same thing. They are afraid of a pain that is already buried deep in their hearts. We may only love awhile, and the ones we love will die.

The play is about savoring the moonlit moment of romantic choice, that place on the dance floor of the heart when two people could kiss, but they haven't yet. You are a dancer and the music is playing like a blue river around you. Everything is in motion and paradoxically, time has ceased its forward motion. And this liquid pulsing photograph of possibilities is placed side by side with mortality, with the certainty of death, with the brevity of youth, with the importance of NOW. *Sailor's Song* is about the almost unbearable beauty of choosing to love in the face of death. Love is the most essential act of courage. Will you choose to love before you are swept away by oblivion? I hope so.

Having lived a life in the theater, I of course hate watching people sit around and talk. What I love is to see people escape the prison of logic and celebrate something deeper, brighter, that territory where sex and the spirit meet. In this play, the boundary between ordinary living and extraordinary display is erased. Characters leap into life on the wings of unexpected music. They turn outward the joy inside so that we can share it. I think there is always a dance going on somewhere. *Sailor's Song* invites you to the dance.

Production History

Sailor's Song was originally produced by LAByrinth Theater Company (John Ortiz and Philip Seymour Hoffman, Co-Artistic Directors)
at The Public Theater (George C. Wolfe, Producer; Mara Manus,
Executive Director) in New York City, opening on November 7, 2004.
It was directed by Chris McGarry; the set design was by Camille
Connolly, the lighting design was by Beverly Emmons, the sound
design was by Elizabeth Rhodes, the costume design was by Mimi
O'Donnell, the choreography was by Barry McNabb and the stage
manager was Christine Lemme. The cast was as follows:

RICH	Danny Mastrogiorgio
JOAN	Katie Nehra
LUCY	Melissa Paladino
JOHN	Stephen Payne
CARLA	Alexis Croucher

Characters

Rich
Joan
Lucy
John
Carla
Jeff (offstage voice)

Place

An American South Atlantic coastal town.

Time

The present.

To the right and left, a bar and a porch. Separating the two, an old boat. Two beautiful girls, Lucy and Joan, one dark and one light, are sitting at a table in the bar. Joan is writing. Lucy, idle and game, is having a drink. The first of the Strauss waltzes plays: "Roses from the South." Mixed in with it we hear a bell buoy ringing. A man in youthful midlife, Rich, enters, sees the girls and they see him. He is Eastern seaboard working-class. He speaks to the audience, and while speaking, comes to sit at the bar, a drink before him. Lucy takes notice of him immediately.

RICH: Everything moves. Emotion. Time. I read in a magazine, they discovered there's a wind that blows through the universe. Goes through the empty and the solid just the same. Like a steady inspiration. Like music. If you could dance with the days of your life, if you could take life by the wrist and dance, I think it would be a waltz. Forward and back, sad and happy, high and low. Picture the ocean. When you stand on a ship on the sea, you feel this music that's in everything, and it hurts like sugar. My name is Rich. I'm going back a few years now. I was in a bar. I was checking out these two bazango-looking girls sitting at a table when one of them came up to me.

(The music continues. Lucy approaches. She has a drink.)

LUCY: What do you like better, the mountains or the beach?
RICH: I like the beach.
LUCY: Right answer.
RICH: Why?
LUCY: 'Cause I like the beach. I'm Lucy.
RICH: Hey, I'm Rich.
LUCY: Good for you.
RICH: No, it's my name.
LUCY: Oh.
RICH: What's your friend writing?
LUCY: That's my sister.
RICH: What's her deal writing on Saturday night in a bar?
LUCY: Why don't you ask her?
RICH: She's busy. I thought I'd ask you.
LUCY: She's not busy.
RICH: She looks busy.
LUCY: Come on. *(They move over to Joan's table)* You from here?
RICH: No. I'm visiting my uncle.

(The music ends. They've arrived at the table. Joan is writing away, but not looking at what she's writing. In fact, she acts like she's not writing.)

LUCY: Joanie, this is Rich.
JOAN: Hey, Rich. How you doin'?
LUCY: He's visiting his uncle.
JOAN: So you're from someplace else.
RICH: That's right.
JOAN: I'm Joan.
RICH: Nice to meet you. I didn't mean to interrupt.
JOAN: You're not interrupting anything. But so your uncle lives around here?
RICH: Sort've. His house is here.
JOAN: Where's he?
RICH: He's here now, but he's a commercial seaman so he's away a lot. My aunt is always here. She's the anchor, he's the, I don't know, bird.

LUCY: And what do you do?

RICH: I'm a commercial seaman, too. He got me in. But he's in it for good and I'm not.

LUCY: You don't like it?

RICH: No, I like it.

JOAN: So . . .

RICH: I've just seen what it did to him, and I don't want that for myself is all.

LUCY: What did it do to him?

RICH: Aaa, he stayed a kid.

LUCY: Is that so bad?

RICH: Depends on your age. He called me once, I hadda post bond to get him out of jail.

JOAN: Whoa.

RICH: I get the call from Argentina: "I'm in a jam, Ritchie!" Don't get me wrong, my uncle's a stand-up guy. And actually, the jail thing was funny if you heard the whole saga. He's really like a hero to me. He's how I ended up on a ship. It's just that I want my life to go another way.

JOAN: And you think you have control over that?

RICH: Somewhat.

JOAN: You're funny.

LUCY: So do you fish?

RICH: No, no. These are container ships. Cargo. I'm a crane operator.

JOAN: You've lived before.

RICH: I have?

JOAN: I think so. I'd have to check.

RICH: With who?

LUCY: So Joan's your type.

RICH: What do you mean?

LUCY: It's all right. She's the more angelic one. I'm like earth.

RICH: You guys are like twenty-four steps ahead of me.

LUCY: Come on. Don't play dumb.

RICH: What's the rush? Do we need to hopscotch to the end of the movie upfront?

LUCY: What kind of movie is it?

RICH: What kind of movie do you go for?

LUCY: Sad.

JOAN: Sad.

RICH: Really?

LUCY: I'm a mush.

JOAN: I like a good cry.

RICH: What's that about?

LUCY: It's about being a girl. What kind of movie do you like?

RICH: Adventure. You know, exotic places, explosions, beautiful women. It's about being a boy. Can I just go to something that's in the forefront here for me? Can I broach something?

LUCY: Sure. Broach away.

RICH: What are you writing?

JOAN: What? This?

RICH: You're writing yards there. What is it?

JOAN: I'm a medium.

RICH: What?

LUCY: Joan's an automatic writer.

RICH: What's that?

JOAN: I allow myself to be possessed by a spirit and the spirit uses me to write.

RICH: What do you mean by "a spirit"? You mean like as in a see-through human being?

LUCY: No. That makes it sound . . .

JOAN *(Overlapping)*: That's right. A ghost.

RICH: Of who?

JOAN: A Punjabi salesman who died in Atlantic City six years ago.

RICH: You're possessed by the ghost of a Punjabi salesman.

JOAN: Just part of me. The arm.

RICH: What'd he sell?

JOAN: Life insurance.

LUCY: You want another drink? What's that, rum and coke?

RICH: Yeah. But you don't have to get me. I should be getting you.

LUCY: Don't resist good fortune. Be right back. *(Goes to the bar)*

JOAN: Is it raining?

RICH: Not yet, but it might I think.

JOAN *(Putting down her pen)*: Who's dying?

(Rich is stricken.)

RICH: What? *(Pause)* My aunt.

JOAN: Don't worry. I'm sorry. I didn't mean to shock you.
You can see the window from where you're sitting. Tell me
if it starts to rain, okay?

RICH: Okay. She's been in a coma for a week. At home. My uncle told
me to get out for a few hours. So it's real? You're a psychic?

JOAN: Yeah.

RICH: Have you always been?

JOAN: I don't know.

RICH: What does the writing . . . What's it about?

JOAN: Heck if I know. It's boring stuff. Like the diary of a person
with a boring life.

RICH: So why do you write it?

JOAN: I don't write it.

RICH: Okay. Why do you . . . let *him* write it using you?

JOAN: He really seems to need to.

RICH: And you're just nice?

JOAN: That's pretty much it.

RICH: Okay. So what's the term again for what you are?

JOAN: I'm an Automatic Writer.

RICH: Cool. You any good at dream interpretation?

JOAN: No.

RICH: I woulda thought you woulda been.

JOAN: Nope.

RICH: 'Cause I keep having this dream.

JOAN: Lay it on me.

RICH: I dream I'm on a couch, I'm in a bed, the point is I'm sleeping. And I dream I'm in a dream. I keep waking up, realizing
I was asleep, and then I wake up again. It goes on like that—
a hall of mirrors—till I'm lost. Till when I really do wake up,
I don't believe it.

JOAN: Even to the point of this? Being here in the bar?

RICH: Hadn't thought a that, but yeah. In a way. Even this. But
there's always a boat, too, at the end of the dream, and it's
leavin', and I don't wanna miss the boat.

JOAN: Yeah, that is a danger. You might miss the boat.

RICH: You think my aunt's gonna die tonight?

JOAN: No.

RICH *(Looks)*: There it is. Drops. It's starting to rain.

(Joan stands up, finishes her drink, and puts her papers away.)

JOAN: Thanks. I'm gonna have to take off. *(Calls)* I'm going, Lucy! It's raining.

RICH: Really?

LUCY *(From the bar)*: Bye. See you at home!

RICH: Where you going?

(She kisses him on the mouth.)

JOAN: Nice to meet you, Rich. We're going to be hanging out I think.

(The door to the bar opens. We hear Jeff. He sounds butch and impatient.)

JEFF *(Off)*: Hey, Joan! You on the way?!

JOAN: Yeah!

(Lucy returns with three drinks in time for Joan's departure.)

LUCY: I'll leave the door unlocked.

JOAN: Oh yeah because the key . . . Okay, good.

RICH: Nice to meet you!

(Joan is gone.)

LUCY: You have to hang out with me now. I have three drinks.

RICH: I can help with that. Damn. Your sister is . . . What is she?

LUCY: Are you being insincere?

RICH: No.

LUCY: Good.

RICH: A little spooked-out. Me I'm talking about.

LUCY: What did she do? Tell you something?

RICH: Something she couldn't know.

LUCY: She does that.

RICH: Who was the guy?

LUCY: Who?

RICH: The guy who didn't come in that she left with.

LUCY: Jeff.

RICH: Who's Jeff?

LUCY: He's this black guy who shows up for her when it rains.

RICH: How's about what?

LUCY: What?

RICH: He shows up when it *rains*?

LUCY: Yeah.

RICH: Where is he when it's not raining?

LUCY: I don't know.

RICH: Look, I'm a routine guy, Lucy. I'm finding it a little challeng-
ing to keep up here sometimes.

LUCY: You're not routine.

RICH: I'm not shockin' the world either.

LUCY: I know what you mean. Look. Just in case you want to know,
let me just put out there something about myself. I'm normal.
I'm a normal person.

RICH: I don't get that. I don't think there's a normal thing about you.

LUCY: I know some girls get off on being told they're amazing. I'm not
one of them. I don't want to be unique. I want to be normal.

RICH: Well, you're up shit's creek. You and your sister are totally
untypical of girls I might meet in a bar.

LUCY: How?

RICH: You could be in a book.

LUCY: What does that mean?

RICH: For one thing your sister is like a secretary to a dead guy.

LUCY: Okay. But that's her. I don't have bizarre stuff like that going
on.

RICH: You've got your sister. And then there's how you look. Beautiful. When I walked in, the music playing . . . You're like a
candelabra on a piano.

LUCY *(Laughs)*: Where do you come up with this stuff?

RICH: Your looks. That come from your parents?

LUCY: My mother's beautiful. My father's handsome, but he has
massive eczema on his face.

RICH: Ow.

LUCY: It's emotional. It's hard for him to say his feelings so they attack him. He's handsome.

RICH: Are your parents like mystical?

LUCY: They're musicians.

RICH: What d'you mean? They have a band?

LUCY: No, they're in an orchestra.

RICH: Oh, that kind.

LUCY: What's your story?

RICH: My story's still being written. I'm thinking about changing a lot of things.

LUCY: Like what?

RICH: Where I live, what I do, my home life.

LUCY: That's a lot.

RICH: Yeah. And then there's just situations you encounter along the way that turn out to be upsetting. You're running along in your own deal and suddenly you're standing next to pain. *(Pause)* You have a very compassionate face.

LUCY: Thank you.

RICH: You look like you care about people.

LUCY: I do.

RICH: That can be overwhelming.

(Rich is distressed.)

LUCY: What's the matter?

RICH: Long day.

LUCY: Oh, you're really . . .

RICH: I'm okay. Sorry.

LUCY: No.

RICH: My aunt is dying.

LUCY: Oh, I'm sorry.

RICH: She's in a coma.

LUCY: Oh! You must be so sad.

RICH: She's dying at home. That's how she wanted it.

LUCY: I understand that.

RICH: It's a *world*, man. The room she's in, it's just a bedroom, but now it's this other universe. You ever hear somebody in a coma *breathe*? It's like a struggling old machine that's gonna give out, but when? You know? So we're just waiting. But she's very strong. She's so strong. She's been like this for a week. I guess it's getting to me.

LUCY: You're close with her?

RICH: No, no, not too close. But it turns out I'm the one who's here. With my uncle.

LUCY: That's what's written down I guess.

RICH: I'm the one who's here.

LUCY: Stuff happens in my life and I always think: So that's what was written down.

RICH: I don't believe in Fate.

LUCY: That's okay. How's your uncle? It's his wife?

RICH: Yeah. He seems completely fine. But she's the whole foundation of this guy. When she goes, my mind tells me that he's got to fall down in a big way. We should talk about something else.

LUCY: Why?

RICH: Why is this a subject for you, right? It's depressing.

LUCY: No, it's not. I like it real.

RICH: You do? I'm not sure I do. I'm a bit of a daydreamer I guess. Don't like it, make up something better. But just the sight of my aunt, like a child, when I got here in that bed . . . I sat there, and her breathing is so forceful . . . It's not that you're in the presence of death. That's what you'd think, but no. It's the other way. You're in the presence of life. And it's big. Bigger than anybody. And it's going to leave. It's like you're waiting for the king to go before everyday things can kick back in. That's a deathbed.

LUCY: I've never had the experience.

RICH: This is my second. My mother was the first. And she was like, the saving grace, you know? That was my wake-up call. Time to change.

(A pause. She kisses him, a lingering kiss. Another pause.)

LUCY: I just broke up with my boyfriend.

RICH: When?

LUCY: As of that kiss.

(He looks at her face.)

RICH: Man.

LUCY: What?

RICH: Pretty.

LUCY: Shut up.

RICH: You've got a little . . .

LUCY: Is something . . . ?

RICH: There's just a touch of shiny . . . like a sparkle . . .

LUCY: Where?

RICH: By your . . . I'll get it. *(Takes out a picturesque old handkerchief)*

LUCY: What's that?

RICH: It's clean.

LUCY: That's not what I mean.

RICH: A handkerchief.

LUCY: It's so pretty!

RICH: You pick these things up in ports. *(Indicating the speck)* Got it. Here.

LUCY: You're giving it to me?

RICH: Sure. It's French.

LUCY: Thank you. I've never been to Europe.

RICH *(Weary)*: I've been everywhere.

LUCY: I'm waiting for some excuse to go.

RICH: Like what?

LUCY: A reason.

RICH: What if no reason comes? What if you're eighty-four years old waiting for a reason to go to Europe?

LUCY: Oh my God, what are you, scaring me?

RICH: Maybe. But this is what scares me, too.

LUCY: But you've been to Europe.

RICH: I've gone all over the world. That's not what I mean. But I didn't find a reason for me anywhere in the sense of my life. A break-through cause. Something that puts me on the other side, you know, with the people who know why they're alive. Am I gonna wait for that to come to me? What if it doesn't come? Or maybe I don't know it when it shows up. Then I'm just another guy waiting to die.

LUCY: You're not that.

RICH: How do you know?

LUCY: I'm looking at you.

RICH: I've got a hot spot in me.

LUCY: Isn't that good?

RICH: What if it's just emotion with nothing behind it in the end? It's gotta be more than that or I'm just suffering through the disappointment of a wasted life. I gotta hope my heart has a face that's gonna like shine out and be clear to me, set me on course like a north star! How great would that be? Not to have to guess about everything. Not to be lost. Why you looking at me like that?

LUCY: You have soul. You shoulda written music, been a professor or something.

RICH: You think so?

LUCY: Sure.

RICH: Ah. School wasn't my thing.

LUCY: I'm not like you. Whatever it is that's going to set my life going, it's out around me somewhere. It's gotta come to me. I'm waiting. I'm a question looking out.

RICH: You think so?

LUCY: Yeah. *(Pause)* I love my handkerchief.

RICH: It looks better in your hand than it ever looked in its life. Wanna walk?

LUCY: Has it stopped raining?

RICH: Yeah.

LUCY: Okay.

(They step outside. Strauss's "Tales from the Vienna Woods" begins to play. They dance out into the night. They are dancing a romantic moonlit walk.)

RICH: The air.

LUCY: The clouds.

RICH: Which way?

LUCY: Doesn't matter.

RICH: Right.

(Lucy laughs with joy.)

What?
LUCY: Nothing! Whee!
RICH: Beautiful!
LUCY: What a night.
RICH: Never forget it.
LUCY: I intend to remember everything!
RICH: Me, too.
LUCY: People are looking.
RICH: Let 'em look.
LUCY: What's happening?
RICH: Magic!
LUCY: I'm a witch!
RICH: Look!

(Lights of a miniature amusement park appear behind them. The ferris wheel turns, and the carousel. Then there are fireworks.)

LUCY: What?
RICH: A ferris wheel!
LUCY: Oh yeah!
RICH: It's a carnival!
LUCY: Lights.
RICH: They're shootin' fireworks!
LUCY: Oh my God! Is it just me?
RICH: No, it's real.
LUCY: I feel this feeling in my heart like . . . like . . . astronomy!
RICH: Yeah! Like we're in the stars.
LUCY: Yeah, like we're dancers in the stars.

(Rich stops, seeing the river before them.)

RICH: And there's the river.
LUCY: Should we jump in?
RICH: End on a high note?
LUCY: You're handsome.

RICH: Your sister.

(They stop dancing. The music continues.)

LUCY: Joan.
RICH: She's very unusual, isn't she?
LUCY: She's amazing.
RICH: I'd better go home.
LUCY: Me, too.
RICH: My uncle's alone. With his wife. That sounds funny.
LUCY: Here's my phone number.
RICH: You work in a bank?
LUCY: That's where the money is. The second number is home.
RICH: Okay. Good night.
LUCY: Good night.

(They part. A step away. He clicks his heels. She flies and leaps. As the music fades, he turns to a porch, where sits his Uncle John. John is ten years older than Rich, salty, tough and charming. He's from somewhere in northern Florida, but he's kicked around for many years. He's got a touch of the pirate about him. Dimly, we hear the steady sound of deep breathing. There's a second chair and a cot on the porch.)

RICH: How is she?
JOHN: The same. She's strong.
RICH: What's with the cot?
JOHN: I took a nap out here. The house smells sick. Did you have any fun?
RICH: I had a very romantic experience. I met these two beautiful women in the bar.
JOHN: Two? I never met *one* woman in that bar.
RICH: Yeah. Sisters. And try this on. One of them is an automatic writer.
JOHN: What's that?
RICH: A medium. She gets possessed and she writes.
JOHN: What about the other one?
RICH: She works in a bank.

JOHN: Which did you like?

RICH: I liked them both. I spent more time with the one who works in the bank. I kissed her. But the other one . . .

JOHN: Forget the other one.

RICH: We shouldn't even be talking about this kind of stuff. Not with Aunt Carla lying there.

JOHN: Don't get righteous on me. My wife is dying. That's bad enough.

RICH: What did you do while I was gone?

JOHN: I drank. I smoked. I try to sit with her but you can't smoke with the oxygen. The hospice worker was by. Talk about hocus-pocus people—these hospice people, they are spooks. So practical about the death and pain. They can look at you and know just how much morphine. I asked her if she believed there is anything after. She said, with the things she's seen, she has no doubt. There are forces, other lives . . . the dead appear to you, speak to you when you are on the point of going. She even mentioned the devil.

RICH: In what way?

JOHN: Just another character who shows up.

RICH: This girl who writes, she's involved with the dead.

JOHN: Well, that doesn't sound good.

(They both laugh.)

RICH: Did you see the rain?

JOHN: Yeah. Here's a drink.

RICH: What's this?

JOHN: Sugar cane brandy from Puerto Rico. Beautiful. Want a cigar?

RICH: I don't smoke, Uncle John.

JOHN: There are no certainties.

RICH: You don't seem very upset.

JOHN: Death is an opportunity to step outside and think. I'm thinking.

RICH: Okay.

JOHN: Two women is very bad.

RICH: Why? What are you talking about?

JOHN: If you like them both. And if you are drawn to novelty, which you are, Ritchie. I know you.

RICH: I don't think you do know me.

JOHN: So you want to be known?

RICH: Sure.

JOHN: Two women. Oh my God! *(Laughs)*

RICH: I'm sorry I told you. You're like an old woman the way you love to go over the gossip.

JOHN: Why you living? To get from here to there? What's the point of that? Is your life just a hurricane and everything behind you wrecked real estate? Your days are nothing till you go back. Significance. You gotta return, under the sun, and find the significance.

RICH: What if there isn't any?

JOHN: The chronicle of life contains many designs. For every man, there are two women. There's the woman you're with, and there's the woman you could be with. Possibility. The certain source of my undoing on many occasions.

RICH: Did she . . . *("Stop breathing?")*

(They both leap to their feet. John looks in an open window on the porch. We hear the breathing resume. He relaxes.)

JOHN: No. She has lungs like a horse.

RICH: She's too young for this to be happening.

JOHN: Tell that to the cancer. Two months ago she had a cough. Now she's in a coma. In a few hours, a week, something, dead. When I went to pick her up at the hospital, she was yelling I was late. And I wasn't by the way. She'd pulled the stuff out, the needles, all that crap. And she was naked to the waist. Yeah! She didn't give a shit. She just wanted to get home. You know what she said while I was getting her in the car? "I have so much work to do!" I got her home and she sank right into a coma. Like a clam closing its shell. And in there, eight days, in whatever Arabian tent a coma is, in there she does her work. While the bellows keep time and the fire burns. And when she's done with her work, she'll die. I have nothing to do with these final things. Thank God I'm here though. What if I had been at sea?

RICH: I know. I missed my mother's . . . It's bad.

JOHN: Don't beat yourself up. You made it for the funeral.

RICH: Yeah.

JOHN: It was hard I know.

RICH: I'm glad I'm here.

JOHN: So am I. Do you think I'm a pig?

RICH: Why would you say that?!

JOHN: Because I screw around and get drunk and even now I'm not shedding tears over my wife's misfortune. Tell me about these two beautiful girls! Will you try to fuck them both?

RICH: Your wife is dying!

JOHN: Tell me I'm wrong. You like the crazy one because she *is* crazy. Right? You like the novelty. It's the same reason you went aboard ship after me. It's not that you like being out on the sea. It's that you like the idea of it. "I am at sea." But I tell you, Ritchie, this romantic song you sing yourself may actually block the voice of God that would guide you to simple happiness.

RICH: Talk about yourself.

JOHN: Me? My story's worse. It starts in the morning. I get up, I do what I like. All day long it goes on the same. I do what I like. But the bitch of it is, the way I like to live moment to moment, day to day, paints up to a picture that's missing something. Adds up to a man . . . Well, a somewhat difficult man. Can I advise you about these girls? You must choose one or you will blow it with both of them. Take the banker! She already kissed you.

RICH: The other one sort've kissed me.

JOHN: What do you mean, "sort've"?

RICH: She kissed me on the mouth with an open mouth.

JOHN: And what did you do?

RICH: It happened so fast I didn't do anything.

JOHN: That's the problem! You have to be so attuned at these unlikely moments or you can't react fast enough to take advantage. Women opening up—it's like a hundred-dollar bill lying in the street on a windy day. Blink and wa-ZAH, the pussy's gone. These are the exact kinds of things that will drive me mad on my deathbed!

RICH: This is what my father says about you.

JOHN: What does he say?

RICH: He says you chase everything and end up with nothing.

JOHN: He says that?

RICH: Yeah.

JOHN: Well, he's right! So take the lesson. Don't chase the two girls and lose them both. Choose one, even the mad one, and let the other go.

RICH: Or what?

JOHN: You'll be forgotten.

RICH: I'm not sure I could get her though, the automatic writer, even if I chose her. She was meeting some black guy.

JOHN: Black?

RICH: Yeah.

JOHN: What is she?

RICH: Blond.

JOHN: So she's an outlaw!

RICH: You could make a living talking out of your ass.

JOHN: You have to admit: It's information.

RICH: That he's black?

JOHN: That he's black and she's blond. She's running from her father!

RICH: I'm going to bed.

JOHN: Do you want me to wake you up if your aunt dies?

RICH: What do you think? Why do you think I'm here?

JOHN: You tell me.

RICH: Yeah, wake me up.

(The lights change, coming up on the boat, as we hear a bell buoy sound. Ottorino Respighi's introduction to "La Prima-vera" from Three Botticelli Pictures *plays. The boat comes alive and sails downstage. Joan and Lucy become passengers; Rich rows. "The Blue Danube" begins playing. It's a sunny day. Lucy has made a choker out of the handkerchief. Joan is in a hat. Rich wears sunglasses. The music continues softly.)*

JOAN: What a beautiful day.

RICH: Perfect.

JOAN: I could hang here forever.

RICH: Me, too.

JOAN: Whose idea was this?

LUCY: Yours.

JOAN: Really? I'm a genius!

LUCY: You don't remember?

JOAN: I remember the first time I tasted ice cream.

LUCY: Right.

JOAN: Rich, isn't Lucy good-looking in the extreme?

RICH: I was just thinking that.

LUCY: You were not.

RICH: Hand to God.

LUCY: How was Jeff?

JOAN: Are you getting tired of rowing, Rich?

RICH: No, I'm loving using my body, the air, the park.
    Jeff. That's the guy shows up when it rains, right? *(The music ends)*

JOAN: Yeah.

RICH: How does that work?

JOAN: We have a connection through the rain.

RICH: So on a day like this . . .

JOAN: No connection. But even when it's raining, it's hard.

RICH: In what way?

LUCY: Jeff is a medium, too.

RICH: He writes?

JOAN: No. In his case, it's full-out possession. The whole body. And he resists so he's like evicted. It's not pretty. Afterwards, he gets so bummed. I'm trying to help him.

RICH: Help him how?

JOAN: Fight off the possession.

RICH: Who's trying to get in?

JOAN: Somebody really bad.

RICH *(Kidding)*: You mean like the devil?

JOAN *(Not kidding)*: I think so.

RICH: You're not kidding.

JOAN: You know what I'm talking about.

RICH: Me? No, I don't know what you're talking about.

LUCY: Maybe we should change the subject.

JOAN: We all contain all the music.

RICH: What's music got to do with it?

JOAN: Everything. Let me ask you something. Do you ever look at the sky and think: I am the sky.

RICH: I'm not sure.

JOAN: Anything can be a mirror. That's just true. You can see yourself in the water.

RICH: Right. Water reflects.

JOAN: I mean more than that.

RICH: More than what?

JOAN: Jeff, me, the water, the devil, Lucy, it's all the same stuff.

LUCY: Leave me out of it.

JOAN: There's no real difference between Lucy and me.

LUCY: Joanie.

JOAN: Or you. You can look at Lucy and see yourself.

RICH: No.

JOAN: Try.

RICH: It's not gonna happen. And the reason is good. When I look at you—and I mean the both of you now—I see like a wonderful country.

LUCY: What country?

RICH: Tahiti.

LUCY: Okay!

RICH: It's sunrise and to starboard there's Tahiti. Land ho.

LUCY: I can live with that. *(To Joan)* We're Tahiti.

JOAN: So what are you?

RICH: Me? I'm *not* Tahiti. That's the point. Come on. Admit it, when you look at me, you don't see a vacation brochure.

JOAN *(Regarding Lucy)*: Don't be so sure.

RICH: I wish I could . . . stop the clock! Before any of this changes. Like Joshua at Jericho. Tell the sun to hold it right there.

JOAN: But it might get better than this.

RICH: But it won't be this.

JOAN: You have to have some faith.

RICH: In what? The future? No. This is the bird in the hand. Right now.

JOAN: You're very Buddhist.

RICH: Buddhist, huh? That would freak my father out. He's born-again.

LUCY: But don't you ever imagine anything in the future?

RICH: Yeah. But it never comes. That's why it's the future.

LUCY: Do you do anything to make it come?

RICH: So far, no. But I want to change that. Come up with a plan. Not today, but soon.

LUCY: That'd be good. Don't wait too long though. 'Cause I'll tell you something. The future comes.

JOAN: What's it like when you're out there on the ocean?

RICH: Aw. Men. A lot of men.

LUCY: Do you have long conversations?

RICH: Sometimes. If we happen to speak the same language. But even if you say the same words, what a man says to a man . . . doesn't give the feeling of comfort. You still would want to tell a woman.

LUCY: Tell a woman what?

RICH: Your secrets. Your pain of life. I shipped with this Russian guy for a while. Nice guy, but a look on his face like he was carrying the national debt. He told me one night about this thing: He called it "the Russian confession."

LUCY: Is this religion?

RICH: No. In the old days in Russia, when a guy was going to propose to a woman, first he confessed to her.

LUCY: Like she was a priest.

RICH: Different.

JOAN: His sins?

RICH: His everything. His past. What hearts he broke. Who broke his heart. His résumé as a dog if you know what I'm saying. So that when he proposed, she had that information, and she would have to forgive him that as part of the deal, take him on in full knowledge. But it was understood that he was saying to her by telling her everything: Because of you I'm not going to do those things anymore. Because of you, I'm going to change.

LUCY: I'm not sure I could deal with that.

RICH: You'd hold it against him?

LUCY: No. I mean the other way. I'm not sure I could tell somebody everything.

JOAN: Sure you could.

LUCY: I think I'd get too embarrassed. My heart'd start beating. I'd blank. I'm not good at like testifying. I bet probably for weeks

after I'd keep saying: Oh, I just remembered another bad
thing I did. The guy would be forgiving me for years.

JOAN: I don't think you've done that much.

LUCY: You don't know everything I've done.

JOAN: But how bad could it be?

RICH: Anyway, what's so bad about add-ons? What would be so bad
about the *habit* of forgiveness between two people?

(This melts Lucy.)

LUCY: Nothing.

JOAN: And if you thought you were going to forget a lot, you could
write it down. You could read it to him. Or you could just
hand him the paper.

LUCY: I'd have to do that.

RICH: I don't think it's supposed to be the woman confessing to the
man though. What I was talking about was the man.

JOAN: But you're talking to women and we see it from the feminine
way.

RICH: You know what though? If you handed me a paper with all
your rap sheet spelled out, I wouldn't read it. I'd just burn it
with a match.

LUCY: Why?

RICH: Chivalry.

JOAN: You'd read it.

RICH: No, you're wrong. I couldn't handle it. I don't wanna know.

JOAN: But you'd want the woman to . . . listen . . . to your stuff.

RICH *(Overlapping)*: Hear me out and forgive me, yes.

LUCY: Then that's not fair.

RICH: I need to think of a woman as being better. I need that. Maybe
it's not realistic but . . . C'mon, you know what I'm saying. You
expect men to be low.

LUCY: But we're not any better.

RICH: You don't know.

LUCY: You don't like men, do you?

RICH: It's not a matter of that.

JOAN: Where's that leave you? You're a man.

RICH: I guess it leaves me looking to women.

LUCY: Don't look at me. I don't know anything. I'm looking for somebody to show me.

RICH: That's not true. You don't know what you bring to the table, but I can see it.

LUCY: What?

RICH: Tolerance.

JOAN: Why does that make me cry?

RICH: Men are hard on each other. Men are stones. Women are the soft shoulder. Otherwise, you know, what's left? Women can accept a man as he is. I'd like to believe that. Even if it's a fairy tale. Do you understand what I'm saying? Do I have to say it out loud? It's embarrassing. I'd like to believe someone on earth could love me.

JOAN: Oh.

LUCY *(Simultaneously)*: Oh.

JOAN: Of course.

LUCY: Rich.

RICH: And it ain't gonna be a man in my case. Women are what men think about when they're at sea. Women are what keep men from jumping in the water. Kindness. I need that. It's the only thing that . . . It's the saving grace.

LUCY: You're so sweet.

JOAN: You need for us to be angels. We'll watch over you. Lucy, especially. Lucy, would you be just so nice to me and sing "Santa Lucia"?

LUCY: No.

JOAN: Oh, don't be like that. Please?

LUCY: I never remember how it starts.

(Joan sings:)

JOAN:

    Now 'neath the silver moon

LUCY:

    Now 'neath the silver moon

JOAN *(For Rich, she quietly points at the sky)*: Think of the sun as the moon.

LUCY: What's the next line?

JOAN:

>Ocean is glowing

>Think of the lake as the ocean *(For Rich, she gently indicates the water)*

LUCY:

>O'er the calm billows
>Soft winds are blowing

JOAN: Whoosh.

LUCY *(Matter-of-factly)*: Shut up, Joan.

>Here stars are dancing low
>All things delight us

>*(Joan joins in.)*

LUCY AND JOAN:

>And as you gently row
>Pure joy invites us
>Hark how the sailor's cry
>Joyously echoes nigh

>Santa Lucia
>Santa Lucia

>Soul of all poetry
>Heart of sweet harmony
>Santa Lucia!
>Santa Lucia!

(As Rich stands, a song like Sergio Franchi's "Lonely Is a Man without Love" kicks in. The girls stand. The boat goes and they, the three of them, dance. A balletic waltz expressing romance among three. Rich is in heaven.)

RICH: Comfy?

JOAN: Yummy.
RICH: Lovely.
LUCY: Sweetheart.
RICH: Am I awake?
JOAN: Who cares?

(Rich has a moment with Joan. Lucy sees it and runs away. Joan pursues her to rejoin the trio. Lucy indicates no, and then relents. The sisters reconcile and rejoin Rich in the dance. Then each woman in turn bids Rich a romantic adieu. Then they are gone. Rich strolls to Uncle John's porch in a romantic dream as the music fades. It is twilight now.)

JOHN: You're shitting me!
RICH: They sang to me! On a boat in the park. "Santa Lucia."
JOHN: That's the sailor's song.
RICH: Yeah?
JOHN: Santa Lucia. That's Saint Lucy.
RICH: What's she the patron saint of?
JOHN: I'd like to think of sailors, since we're sailors.
RICH: You're a sailor. I'm . . .
JOHN: You're a sailor, too.
RICH: No, with me it's just a temporary solution.
JOHN: Okay. *(Referring to the breathing)* Can you hear it? She's congested now. You can hear the water.
RICH: Can they do anything?
JOHN: They can drain it, kind of a vacuum thing, but they tell me it'll come back in a couple of hours. No. She's done for.
RICH: Ten days of this.
JOHN: Poor Carla. I wonder what she's doing in that dark place. I wonder if she makes the shadows of the past stand up and act it all out. Or if it's about God. I just hope it's not about our shitass bit of wedlock. Two months a year. That's all she got for the grief it gave. Two months. No children.
RICH: How you doing?
JOHN: I don't know. I've never had such a period of reflection on land. Always before it was on the sea. Let me hold your hand.

(Rich sits beside his uncle, lets his uncle take his hand.)

I never meant to stop like this. So long. If this keeps up . . . *(Lets Rich's hand go)* Your hand's no good. *(Suddenly fierce)* She's got to go soon!

RICH: Take it easy.

JOHN: What's she doing?

RICH: How did you two come to marry?

JOHN: She got pregnant.

RICH: Oh. I didn't know.

JOHN: That's because she lost the baby right after the wedding. So we didn't have to get married, there was no point, but we'd already done it. I met her in Europe you know? I was bumming down the Danube, doing some short hops, freight work. I met her at a concert in Germany. This soul singer sang this song. She stood up, she started dancing. Man, she could dance! But alone you know? American girl! What a piece of ass! I was too old for her. I knew there was only one way to bag her. I had to fuck her until she got pregnant.

RICH: Were you sad when the . . . when she lost the baby?

JOHN: A bit.

RICH: Are you sad now?

JOHN: I guess.

RICH: I don't understand you.

JOHN: No?

RICH: Not really.

JOHN What don't you understand?

RICH: Does anything touch you?

JOHN: What moves you?

RICH: Plenty.

JOHN: Name something.

RICH: When Lucy sang. That touched me.

JOHN: Her singing touched you, not her. You are moved by ideas. You're like me. You're worse than me.

RICH: I'm very different than you.

JOHN: I'm the realistic one at this stage of the game. You fell in love with the stars, with faces in clouds, when you were a kid I guess.

No part a you's come back to realism yet. At least I got a foothold. You think you're like your father?

RICH: In some ways.

JOHN: I'm looking at you.

RICH: What's that mean?

JOHN: I'm your lighthouse, buddy. You think it was me encouraged you to go to sea?

RICH: Well yeah. I mean, I needed a job, you helped me out . . .

JOHN: You were always at sea.

RICH: You don't know the first thing about me.

JOHN: Sometimes I wonder if you live completely in a fucking coloring book, Ritchie. Don't you know the base truth of anything?

RICH: What are you talking about?

JOHN: You. I don't know you? Are you kidding? You're my guy. I love you.

RICH *(Embarrassed)*: Thanks.

JOHN: Always have.

(Rich doesn't know what to do with that.)

RICH: Okay.

JOHN: I've made you uncomfortable.

RICH: No.

JOHN: You think you need to keep me out.

RICH: No. Why would I? Absolutely not.

JOHN: Shit. You're looking at me like a bug. It's all so stupid.

RICH: I don't understand what—

JOHN *(Overlapping)*: We're both right here but it's like we're on two different mountains.

RICH: I'm right here.

JOHN: No, Ritchie, you are not right here! You are in the fucking counting house running your fingers through your shitass inheritance. And what's that? Your father's attitude. Ignorance is passed down in some families like a gold watch. There's a hole in the ground between us. Neither one of us dug it, but you gotta take a chance on me, buddy. Otherwise, it's just you and your dad.

RICH: Let's leave my dad out of this.

JOHN: Can't. He's here.

RICH: No, he's in Orlando in a time-share reading the Bible!

JOHN: I turn your father's stomach. When I touched his hand, it made him sick. When I told him I loved him, it disgusted him. Like I was something rotten. Always, every time. He was my brother! But I might as well have been a dog trying to get up on him. He made me feel like a freak because I had tenderness.

RICH: He's okay.

JOHN: And what about me? Am I okay?

RICH: Sure.

JOHN: And what about you, how are things with you?

RICH: Fine.

JOHN: You think I'm an asshole, don't you?

RICH: No.

JOHN: Well, I'm going to tell you something. It's a curse to be invisible and it can be a curse to love. A curse. I recognize you, but you don't see me at all.

RICH: What are you talking about? I'm looking right at you. I've known you all my life. I see you fine!

JOHN: No. But I see you.

RICH: Well, there's nothing to say if you're not gonna listen.

JOHN: There's plenty to say, but you won't talk. You and I, we are not made of the same things as some other people, Ritchie. You've got to understand that or they'll hurt you too much.

RICH: Nobody's hurting me.

JOHN: Do you hurt? Are you going to lie to me? It's part of your face.

RICH: Okay, okay.

JOHN: You think it's me. You think you're keeping *me* out. That I'm beating on your door. That's the joke. What you don't see is YOU'RE THE DESPERATE ONE!

RICH: What does that mean?! I'll tell you what I think. I think you're looking for somebody to agree with you against my dad. You're looking for me to tell you you're right and he's wrong. Typical family shit. Well, guess what? I don't think either of you are right! If you got a beef with him, call him! It has nothing to do with me.

JOHN: Maybe. Nothing is certain. You know that, Ritchie. In your secret soul you know that. But come on, enough, *qué pasa*? Did you fuck either of these girls yet?

RICH: What's the matter with you?!

JOHN: I changed the subject. Isn't that what you wanted?

RICH: Why do you have to drag everything through the mud?!

JOHN: What do you have against mud?

RICH: What about beauty? What about beautiful things?

JOHN: God took mud and made you. He breathed on it. Maybe His breath stank, but without the breath, where would you be?

RICH: But shouldn't life have poetry?

JOHN: It does! But it's good poetry! Not the white doughnut chitchat at a church breakfast. Blood! Shit! Awful things! And anyway, beware poetry of all kinds! You! If you have some fantasy of stepping ashore and leaving the fantastic behind. Out there rowing your boat in the park with those mermaids singing to you. What is that, Sinbad? Remember! Beauty fades! It perishes. It can't be held! *(It's about his wife now)* She's dying. Tonight's the night.

RICH: You think so?

JOHN: Yes. I will sit with her now till it comes. Will you sit with me?

RICH: Of course.

JOHN *(Standing)*: Then open that cot, Ritchie. Goddamnit, I promised myself she would not die in that stinkin' room.

(John goes in the house. Rich opens the cot on the porch. John reappears with a tiny little woman wrapped in a sheet in his arms.)

She weighs nothing. Get the oxygen tube and run it through the window. It should be long enough.

RICH: Sure.

(Rich goes in as John lays the woman on the cot, murmuring to her all the while.)

JOHN: That's right, Carla. That's right. What did they do to you? Beautiful girl. You always liked the porch. It will be easier for the angels to find you here.

(Rich appears at the window with the oxygen tube and hands it to John.)

RICH: Here it is. There's no problem. It reaches.

JOHN: Thank you, Ritchie. *(Puts it under her nose)* There you go. That fucking chemotherapy. Ritchie, bring out that brandy, would you?

RICH: Sure. *(He disappears from the window)*

JOHN: Oh my God, it's impossible that this could be you, Carla. It's not possible.

(Rich comes out with a couple of glasses and the bottle of brandy. John is lighting the stub of a cigar.)

RICH: You're not supposed to smoke around the oxygen.

JOHN: I will though. Have you ever heard of an oxygen explosion? Ridiculous bullshit designed to terrify the ignorant. I will not live in fear! Right, Carla?

RICH: You think she can hear you?

JOHN: The hospice worker said yes, but I don't know. Look at her. To my eye, she's got the brain scan of a head a lettuce.

RICH: I can't make up my mind whether you are horrible or good.

JOHN: Don't make up your mind. *(Pause)* So if you don't intend to stay a sailor, what are you going to do? *(Pause)*

RICH: I'd like to be a psychiatrist.

JOHN: A psychiatrist?!

RICH: I think I could be good at it.

JOHN: You know that's an M.D.? You'd have to go through the whole thing of medical school to become a doctor, and then the whole course of practice to become a psychiatrist.

RICH: No, I don't mean a psychiatrist then, I mean a therapist. You don't have to do all that to be a therapist.

JOHN: What do you have to do to be a therapist?

RICH: Rent a room. Hang a sign.

JOHN: A therapist of what?

RICH: You know, the mind. People.

JOHN: Fuck a duck. Why?

RICH: I think it'd be interesting. I think I could give good advice. Make some money.

JOHN: You?

RICH: Yeah, me.

JOHN: But you don't know anything.

RICH: Yes, I do. I've talked to people and they've found me very helpful.

JOHN: What people?

RICH: Buddies, girls I know.

JOHN: You know, Ritchie, I'm glad we're having this conversation because I had no idea how big a horse's ass you are. Carla, count your blessings baby you're unconscious. Your nephew has the I.Q. of an avocado. Give me a drink, you freaking widget, please.

RICH: I'm not going to talk to you if you're going to be discouraging.

JOHN: How old are you? Don't tell me. You're no kid. What are you doing talking like you're in high school?

RICH: I could become a therapist.

JOHN: You're a man, you've gone through doors that shut behind you, bang, you are someone. You are not at the start of things.

RICH: I still could do anything!

JOHN: No.

RICH *(Regarding himself)*: It's all in your mind.

JOHN: What are you talking about?! Time is not in your mind, death is not in your mind. What is this, positive thinking? *(Referring to Carla)* This is death. Death is real. The end. Do you think Carla is lying here thinking: Maybe I'll take an acting class? The scenarios are limited, Ritchie. One can do many things, but one cannot do everything, and the clock is ticking. You've put down ten years towards your retirement, you need another ten. What? Now you think you're going to start again with something new and that's going to make you young? No.

RICH: Are you happy you stayed working on ships?

JOHN: Yes!

RICH: Bullshit!

JOHN: I'm happy I stuck it out somewhere, doing something! This is the same thing you're having with these girls. You won't choose. But time waits for no one, my friend. And either you fuck the one and not the other, or you fuck them both, or one day soon you will never fuck them, you will be prevented from fucking them by time, by temperament, by chance, and they will vanish! Except in your mind. Where they will dance like teasing devils on your deathbed. *(To Carla)* Is that what you're doing, baby? Seeing the other men you might've married had you not fucked me? *(To Rich)* Fate.

RICH: I don't believe in Fate.

JOHN: It's not necessary for you to believe.

RICH: You shouldn't tell anybody anything.

JOHN: That's true.

RICH: My father says you're a failure.

JOHN: My brother said that?

RICH: Yeah.

JOHN: Prick. Why was your father's course the right one? Because he has a son? So what? You're going to die, too. Children change nothing. It still all ends in bones.

RICH: Maybe it's not the end that matters.

JOHN: I hope not. You're losing some of your hair. I hate to see that. I'm telling you, Ritchie, bang these girls quick before they get realistic.

RICH: Give me a drink.

JOHN: This stuff was given me by a Brazilian Puerto Rican Jewish girl with a face like the moon in the jungle.

RICH: Did you fuck her?

JOHN: No, she got away!

(They laugh.)

RICH: If I want to think about becoming a therapist without getting all practical about it upfront, you shouldn't make fun of me.

JOHN: You're right.

RICH: That's how things get real. First you dream, then you get practical.

JOHN: That's true.

RICH: You know what else I thought of getting into?

JOHN: Tell me.

RICH: Politics.

JOHN: Politics.

RICH: You don't have any kind of college or anything to be involved in politics. Behind the scenes, whatever, you know.

JOHN: You could fuck the mayor's wife.

RICH: Can't you be serious for a minute?

JOHN: I am serious. That would be behind the scenes. There's the mayor on TV and you at home, behind the scenes, fucking his wife.

RICH *(Struggling to communicate the truth of his life)*: Look! I need something. You're right. I'm not perfectly young anymore and I feel my life melting away into just a pot of days with nothing to show. You want me to talk about my father? It's too late to talk about my father and me, what it might have been. How much it hurts. Who cares? I gotta put that behind me. I'm struggling in my own deal now. Yes, I have pride! But it needs a name! Who am I? I'm proud, but why?! The time has come. I have to be able to name a reason!

JOHN: There are real things that prevent despair.

RICH: Well, that's what I'm trying to get.

JOHN: You don't get that from a job.

RICH: Then what?

JOHN: Be here, Ritchie. Be with me. Be with us.

(A quiet descends. A long moment. The breathing becomes louder. Carla thrashes suddenly, and chokes loudly. John and Rich leap up, try to comfort her, restrain her. Music: A song like Otis Redding singing "Try a Little Tenderness" from his Live in Europe *album. She falls back. She's dead. They assume quiet attitudes of grief. The song gains momentum. Carla rises, dressed in white. It is her spirit, free of burden. She dances in the white sheet. First she's a girl holding her father's hand, then a tomboy, then a young woman feeling attractive for the first time, then wildly sexual and free, free! Then in rebellion! She has torn off the sheet. She's in a short dress. John approaches her, attracted, tries to embrace her. She shoves him violently away. He tries again, with the same result. Then she goes to him in simple surrender. He kisses her. She collapses. She's dead. She's gone. John lifts her up. He carries her away. The music continues.*

During this, Rich has put on a loose tie and jacket. The lights change. An outdoor café table at night. Little white lights. Mandolin music comes on: "Mattinata." Rich has a drink. Lucy appears. She has the handkerchief on her wrist now. She has a drink, too. They dance, pleasantly weary, a little drunk.)

LUCY: Are you relieved?

RICH: I don't know what I am.

LUCY: How's your uncle?

RICH: My uncle? Get this. He wants to meet you and Joan.

LUCY: Well, that's nice.

(They stop dancing.)

RICH: Tonight! He buried his wife this morning and he wants to party with some girls tonight!

LUCY: Really.

RICH: He said he wants to get out.

LUCY: I guess that makes sense.

RICH: You're very nice, Lucy. You're nicer than me.

LUCY: I know. That's how you see it. *(He shakes his head)* I like you.

RICH: Why? How? What about me do you like?

LUCY: I like who you are.

RICH: Who am I? Not very much, right? I mean, I've got a heartbeat but what makes me worth anything? Nothing.

LUCY: You're upset.

RICH: Goddamn right. Drunk too. A little.

LUCY: Your aunt died.

RICH: It's not that.

LUCY: Then what's bothering you?

RICH: Stuff.

LUCY: Do you like Joan better than me? *(No answer)* You know what I think? I think you believe a woman would have to be crazy to love you and Joanie's crazy.

RICH: You're calling your sister crazy?

LUCY: Yes, I am. Do I love her, yes. Do I want to believe her, yes. Do I believe her? No.

RICH: But you always seem like you do.

LUCY: That's love. I'm not going to fight. I'm just going to hope and pray that someday she comes back.

RICH: But she does say psychic stuff that's true.

LUCY: The news that she can see around a corner once in a while doesn't make her sane. I'm not saying this because I want to ruin her for you. It's just that you'd be making a mistake. And then there's that other thing.

RICH: What?

LUCY: Me. *(Pulls out a sheet of paper)* I wrote it down.

RICH: What?

LUCY: My confession.

RICH: What are you talking about? No.

LUCY: Everything. It was hard to write. It's hard to be honest. There was more than I thought. I want you to read it.

RICH: I told you. I don't want to know those things.

LUCY: You think that women are better than you, but we're all just people.

RICH: But we're not all the same. I don't want us all to be the same.

LUCY: Why not?

RICH: 'Cause if everybody's like me then there's no help.

LUCY: Love isn't being saved by an angel. It's really different than that.

RICH: I don't want to read it. I wouldn't be able to forget it then.

LUCY: It's just ordinary things. Take it.

RICH: No.

LUCY: I want you to know me. I want someone to know me.

RICH: I don't want to know you! Okay? I don't want you to be real!

LUCY: I am real!

RICH: I don't want any of this to be real.

LUCY: Look. Touch my face. Real. *(Takes his hand and touches it to her cheek)* See?

RICH: If you're real . . . then nothing lasts.

LUCY: Well, that's true, isn't it?

RICH: No. I can't take it. *(Hands her back her confession)* Tear it up.

LUCY: No.

RICH: Look . . .

JOHN *(Off)*: Ritchie!

RICH: Hey. *(To Lucy)* It's my Uncle John.

(John appears in a jacket and tie. He's had a drink or two, but he's in pretty good shape. He's carrying a bottle of champagne.)

LUCY: Hi.

JOHN: My wife died.

LUCY: I'm sorry.

JOHN: You must be Lucy.

RICH: Uncle John, this is Lucy.

JOHN: Beautiful to meet you.

LUCY: I'm so sorry about your wife.

JOHN: Thank you. Honestly. You ever have anybody die?

LUCY: No.

JOHN: It's the weirdest. Champagne?

LUCY: Sure.

JOHN: Ritchie?

RICH: I'm good.

JOHN: Ritchie is not approving of the way I grieve.

RICH: Is that what you're doing?

(Joan enters. John looks at her with appreciation.)

LUCY *(To Rich)*: How you doing?

JOHN: And you must be Joan.

JOAN: Hi. Yeah.

JOHN: Like a poem written in my soul with the blood of my body in the secret language of my heart.

JOAN: Oh my God. How beautiful.

JOHN *(Regarding Joan)*: Just what I was thinking.

JOAN: I'm sorry about your wife.

JOHN: Thank you. She is . . . under the ground. As of this morning. Glass of champagne?

JOAN: Thanks.

RICH: Most people don't serve champagne at a funeral.

JOHN: The funeral's done.

RICH: Some people grieve for years.

JOHN: To each his own. I am not a conventional person. I'm a sailor.

LUCY: Is that like the military?

JOHN: No. Commercial. Cargo ships. They require a crew. I'm an engineer. Ritchie operates a very impressive crane. It can lift thousands of pounds of freight.

LUCY: Wow!

RICH: Who would care about a thing like that! I work a crane. Big deal. A kid could do it.

JOHN: He undervalues his own accomplishments. There are upwards of twenty controls on this crane the operation of which is no mean thing.

RICH: Are you really doing this?

JOHN: What?

RICH: Are you trying to use your wife's death to pick up girls?

JOAN: Be cool, Rich.

RICH: No, it's disgusting!

JOHN: More importantly, do you think it will work?

RICH: Everything my father said about you is true, isn't it?

JOHN: I think it's probably more important what he says about you.

RICH: Lay off that!

JOHN: Why? If there's nothing there, there's nothing there. What does my fine fat brother say about you? *(No answer)* I thought so. I'm waiting for you, Ritchie. So Joan, I understand you are a spiritualist of some kind? You do automatic writing?

JOAN: So Rich told you.

JOHN: Of course.

RICH: You're waiting for me to what?

(John makes his demand. It's a showdown.)

JOHN: Console me.

(Rich makes his demand.)

RICH: For what? Show me something!

(Awkward silent struggle. It's a standoff.)

LUCY *(Taking Rich's hand)*: You wanna go somewhere?

RICH: I'm fine.

(John drops his demand.)

JOHN *(To Rich)*: Afraid to leave us alone? *(To Joan)* I knew an automatic writer in Paraguay. One must be intensely sensitive. She used to tell me: "I feel it in my ass."

RICH: You never knew any automatic writer!

JOHN: Oh but I did, Ritchie.

RICH: Why didn't you mention it?

JOHN: I didn't want to lessen your achievement in having met one. I have known three automatic writers.

RICH: Man, you will just say anything.

JOAN: I guess I don't understand what's at issue here.

LUCY: Rich, come on, don't fight.

RICH: I'm not fighting. I'm just amazed. I'm sorry, Uncle John. I know somewhere in there this is a terrible terrible day for you and you should be however you want. But I just don't understand you at all.

JOAN: Maybe you guys need some time alone?

JOHN: Absolutely not! If you leave me with him, he will kill me.

RICH: Is everything a joke to you?

JOHN: Is the man with the serious tone more honest? Is sobriety itself a demonstration of the truth of something? Or are you just proud of the ditch you've dug around your house? Are you proud of your strength, Ritchie? Is the man who succeeds in hiding his heart stronger than the soldier of many battles staggering in the open field? Who is true? What is right? Who needs the help of God more? I don't know.

(To Joan) Tell me something, Joan. Do you believe that we have lived before?

JOAN: Oh yeah.

JOHN: Because I swear to God this is not the first time we've met! And what's more, it's my instinct that we were parted against our will, at the behest of others, in an ancient setting. Perhaps Egypt. When the fabric to the other world was pulled aside for my wife, I was there, and I saw the outline of fabulous things. It was very comforting and it gave me courage to accept what visions come to me. I'm telling you. I recognize you. I know you. From long ago.

JOAN: You look a little familiar to me, too.

RICH: He just wants to fuck you.

LUCY: Ritchie!

RICH: He'll say anything.

JOHN: My nephew is going through a personal crisis. I hope you can forgive him.

RICH: What crisis?

JOHN: He's like me.

RICH: I'm nothing like you.

JOHN: But he hates himself.

RICH: I'm not like you!

JOHN: I don't blame him for wanting it to be different. For dreaming of more while his actual life rots in the rain. But he can only run away into a waste of nothing. Loneliness. *(To Rich)* Who are you like? Your father? I don't think so.

> *(To Joan)* Maybe we two should leave these two. They'll have a better time on their own. We could go down by the river. Would you consider it? My wife just died and I need to talk.

JOAN: Yeah, we could do that.

RICH: Joan, are you actually falling for this ridiculous line of shit? I can't believe it! C'mon.

(Rich is looking to her, appealing to her. Joan looks into his eyes and sees the future.)

JOAN: You want what you don't want. You want to know what I see? There's an arrow in your stomach. If you pull it out, you think you'll bleed to death. If you don't pull it out, there's an arrow in your stomach. There will never be anything between you and me of a romantic nature.

RICH: Don't say that.

JOAN: I've said it.

RICH: How can you be sure?

LUCY: I know when I'm beat.

(Lucy tears up her confession. Joan pats Rich's arm. Maybe he pulls his away. And then Joan turns to John.)

JOAN: Would you like to talk to your wife?

JOHN: What do you mean?

LUCY: Joanie?

(Joan ignores her and continues to John.)

JOAN: Your wife is here. She wants to use me. Do you want to speak to her?

(Pause.)

JOHN: No.

(Joan is being possessed.)

JOAN: Too late.

LUCY: Joanie, don't.

JOAN: She's coming. I'm here.

(Joan stiffens as she is entered by a spirit. She walks to John, regards him.)

John. John.

(She kisses him passionately. He responds, and then shoves her violently away. He is beside himself, horrified, frightened.)

JOHN: Get the fuck away from me! Get the fuck away! What are you doing?! I'll kill you! *(Rich restrains him)* Do you understand, you witch! Take your sister and get the fuck out of here!

RICH: Easy!

JOHN: Take her away, get her away, I tell you!

(Lucy has her sister, who's now vulnerable. She leads her away.)

LUCY *(To Rich)*: She didn't mean it.

RICH: I'm sorry. *(Grabs his uncle)* Hey, man, what are you doing?

(Music: An attenuated version of "The Blue Danube" begins to play. It is the long-held-back grief of this man. John starts to break down.)

JOHN: Oh my God, Oh my God. My wife of many years is dead. She *is* here, and I can't have her. Not ever again.

RICH: Hey. Hey. John. Nothing is certain. That's all we know.

(They are on the ground. Rich is comforting John, frightened that he may be looking at himself.

Carla appears. John senses her and stands. The meat of the waltz begins. John and Carla waltz.

Lucy comes back and starts to waltz with Rich. Joan reenters at a run, taps Lucy on the shoulder, cutting in. Joan and Rich waltz as Lucy walks away, a victim of unrequited love. Lucy takes off Rich's handkerchief and tosses it, letting it float to the ground. She's gone.

Carla kisses John and exits. Joan kisses Rich and exits. The two men are alone and bittersweet. They look at each other, and then John raises his hands for Rich to come to him. They embrace. The music dominates. They walk slowly off, arm in arm.)

END OF PLAY